GARDEN TO TABLE

COOKBOOK

Garden to Table Cookbook is an original work, first published in 2023 by Fox Chapel Publishing Company, Inc.

Project Team
Managing Editor: Gretchen Bacon
Editors: Jeremy Hauck and Sherry Vitolo
Acquisitions Editor: Amelia Johanson
Designer: Chris Morrison
Photographer: Rachel Benavides
Indexer: Jay Kreider
Proofreader: Kurt Conley

Images from Shutterstock.com: VasilkovS (vegetable illustrations throughout book); mythja (2); kram-9 (11); PriceM (10); kram-9 (11); Fevziie (18); 13Smile (20); Alexander Raths (28–29); Peangdao (30–31); Stanislav Stradnic (32–33); Taras Grebinets (34); Shchus (35); successo images (40); Julia-Bogdanova (42); Zigzag Mountain Art (49); Brent Hofacker (56–57, 174, 175); Lilly Trott (80–81); Rimma Bondarenko (122–23); Yulia Gust (154); Marie Sonmez Photography (162–63)

ISBN 978-1-4971-0292-7 (paperback)
ISBN 978-1-4971-0410-5 (hardcover)

Library of Congress Control Number: 2022949756

Fox Chapel Publishing
903 Square Street
Mount Joy, PA 17552

To learn more about the other great books from Fox Chapel Publishing, or to find a retailer near you, call toll-free 800-457-9112 or visit us at *www.FoxChapelPublishing.com*.

We are always looking for talented authors. To submit an idea, please send a brief inquiry to acquisitions@foxchapelpublishing.com.

Printed in China
First printing

GARDEN TO TABLE
COOKBOOK

A Guide to Growing, Preserving, and Cooking What You Eat

Kayla Butts

Master of Science, Registered Dietitian Nutritionist, Licensed Dietitian

Photography by Rachel Benavides

Fox Chapel
PUBLISHING

Spring

Summer

CONTENTS

Fall

Winter

INTRODUCTION: CONNECTING YOUR HEALTH TO THE SOIL

Garden to Table Cookbook is for everyone. Whether you're already growing and eating your own food or just interested in doing so, you'll find valuable information for taking home-grown or locally grown foods and turning them into beautiful, tasty dishes to nourish your body and soul.

The benefits of aligning your eating habits with a more earth-centered, less chemical-laden process are endless. When I began growing and preserving my own food, I truly learned how cultivation and garden-to-table living feeds mind, body, and spirit.

Embracing garden-to-table eating can truly change your life. In this introduction, I'll explore the reasons why. We'll start by walking through my nutrition journey, from my first experiences with the power of food, through my traditional instruction, to my real-world education. Then I'll dive into the facts—providing insights into the research and explaining why embracing locally sourced and homegrown foods is so important and the benefits of growing your own food.

After that, I'll give you practical tools you can use to change your eating habits. You'll jump into the three main techniques for preserving fruits and vegetables and find both my favorite healthful canning recipes and a detailed Storage and Preservation Chart to help you start your preservation journey off on the right foot.

Finally, we'll end with the best part—recipes for wholesome, colorful, nourishing dishes organized by season so you can make the most of your harvests throughout the year! Let's get started.

Finding Joy in My Journey to Health

I started growing and preserving my own food to support my husband's farming business, but I continued to garden, preserve, and cook, through 100-degree summers, barren winters, and a devastating hurricane, to find something greater. Working the land, savoring the fruits of my labor, and sharing my harvest with loved ones led to fulfillment and the discovery of my best self. I learned how to nourish my mind, body, and spirit through feeding my family. Join me on this journey to find your best health, fulfillment of your land, and contentment for your soul.

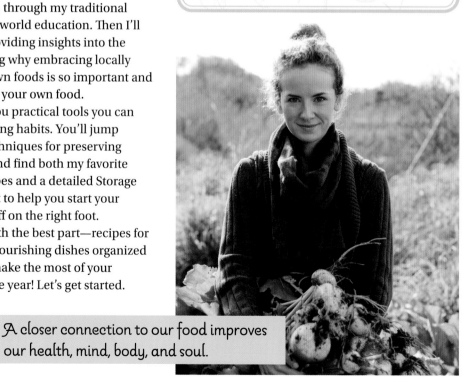

A closer connection to our food improves our health, mind, body, and soul.

It is tremendously satisfying to harvest vegetables you've grown yourself.

The Right Food Can Save Your Life

I was seven years old when I first began to realize that food was the answer. It was a hot, humid afternoon at the Houston Zoo and my mom had just experienced her first grand mal seizure.

In the following months, I watched her undergo a battery of tests, consult a team of specialists, and consider brain surgery. She was finally diagnosed with epilepsy—an ambiguous diagnosis for pretty much any baffling seizure disorder.

"My mom's recovery forever cemented the power of food in my mind."

Her doctors couldn't explain the causes or offer solutions. She was prescribed anticonvulsants, antidepressants, and anti-epileptic drugs. She became depressed, gained weight, lost her hair, and eventually broke down.

At her wit's end, she did some research on her own and found a controversial option—the ketogenic diet. Her dietitian explained to her that a ketogenic diet is low in carbs and sugar, and high in protein and fat. We had scrambled eggs, bacon, and unsweetened grapefruit juice for breakfast. We had salad with boiled eggs and cheese for lunch and a low-carb dinner.

The weight gain stopped. The seizures stopped. She has been seizure-free for over twenty-five years now. Where prescription drugs had failed, food triumphed. My mom's recovery forever cemented the power of food in my mind.

> *"Within six months of eating food free of chemicals and grown by hands I knew, I lost fifteen pounds, my hormones leveled out, and I had a much deeper appreciation for the delicious taste of truly unadulterated food."*

My Nutrition Education

I struggled with my own weight for many years. I was "one of the big kids" in my elementary class, gained ten pounds in a matter of months during my senior year of high school, gained the typical freshman fifteen in college, and by sophomore year of college I was classified as overweight. (Have I mentioned that I hate the BMI classification system? Well, I do.)

After college, I followed the traditional dietary dictums. I ate lean protein, avoided too much fat, and focused on fruits and vegetables. I exercised four to five days per week, running three to four miles, biking six to ten miles, and spending hours at the gym. I was doing everything right, but I continued to struggle with maintaining my weight.

I had a master's degree in nutrition and had been working and studying in the field for almost a decade when my *true* food education began. My view on food changed when I met my husband. He served me a bacon burger made from grass-fed beef, pastured bacon, and tomatoes all grown on his farm. Within six months of eating food free of chemicals and grown by hands I knew, I lost fifteen pounds, my hormones leveled out, and I had a much deeper appreciation for the delicious taste of truly unadulterated food.

There are many benefits to growing vegetables at home—including creating a sense of connection with the world around you.

The Standard American Diet (SAD)

It doesn't take a nutritionist to see there's something wrong within our food system. More than two-thirds of Americans are overweight and researchers estimate less than 3 percent of the US population is considered to have a "healthy lifestyle."[1] The Standard American Diet involves consuming an excess of inflammatory fats, sugar, and salt, and a lack of fiber from fruits and vegetables. Perhaps most disturbing is that even the nutrient-dense foods in our food system lack the nutrition they should have.

The majority of health concerns in America today (certain types of diabetes, heart disease, certain cancers, high blood pressure, high cholesterol, and on and on) all have one thing in common—they can often be prevented. Eating more nutritious stuff while cutting back on disease-promoting foods does the trick.[2]

As most of us can testify, it's not easy. There are dozens of factors working against our efforts to improve our health. Demanding work and home lives leave us scrambling for convenient food options and many of us now have jobs where we're sitting most of the day.

An unspoken cause of the obesity epidemic is the chemicals often saturating our foods. Take the healthiest foods available in the supermarket—fruits and vegetables. They are often sprayed with herbicides like atrazine (a substance banned in Europe), wrapped in plastics containing phthalates, and cooked in nonstick pans that contain perfluorooctanoic acid. These tongue-twisting chemicals are classified by experts as "obesogens"—chemicals that promote weight gain.

These chemicals combined with the lack of nutrient density in much of our soil create a perfect storm for lower health. All of the vitamins, minerals, and micronutrients a plant contains are absorbed through the soil it is grown in. The herbicides, fungicides, pesticides, and synthetic fertilizers applied to commercial crops kill off much of the microbial life necessary for increasing the nutrient content of the soil.

Many crops are picked before they have had a chance to absorb adequate amounts of vitamins and minerals from the soil. These fruits and vegetables are then stored in warehouses and shipped long distances, losing vital nutrients along the way.

The inefficiency of this system has significant consequences: depleted topsoil, produce lacking in nutrients, and a huge carbon footprint. The Food and Agriculture Organization (FAO) of the United Nations in 2015 estimated that over 90 percent of the topsoil on Earth would be devoid of nutrients by the year 2050.[3]

The aim of our current agricultural system is to grow as much food as possible in as little time as possible. Taste, environmental considerations, and nutrition don't always factor into "big ag" consideration.

> "It doesn't take a nutritionist to see there's something wrong within our food system."

> "Demanding work and home lives leave us scrambling for convenient food options and many of us now have jobs where we're sitting most of the day."

"As neurosurgeon and health advocate Dr. Sanjay Gupta puts it, 'If we are what [we] eat, Americans are corn and soy.'"

Commodity Crops and the Fall of the Family Farm

The 1950s–1970s was a turning point for the American food system. Americans began to value convenience and technology over homemade and handmade. Farm families sold their land to work in factories or businesses in town.

After World War II, the agricultural sector saw a tremendous rise in the use of synthetic pesticides, herbicides, and fertilizers. At the same time, the government started to provide generous incentives for commodity crops, like corn and soybeans. Food scientists invented products like high fructose corn syrup, the soy derivative textured vegetable protein (TVP), and partially hydrogenated oils to use up any excess crops.

Fast-forward to now, and almost all of our processed foods include corn, soy, or both. As neurosurgeon and health advocate Dr. Sanjay Gupta puts it, "If we are what [we] eat, Americans are corn and soy."[4]

Poor Dirt: How Unhealthy Soil Leads to Fewer Vitamins and Minerals in Today's Produce

As a dietitian, my job is to help people figure out what to eat to improve their health and get all the nutrients they need from food. Simple, right? I started my practice thinking I could give clients a meal plan heavy on fruits and veggies and my job would be done. Wrong! Turns out, it takes a LOT more of "the good stuff" nowadays to get the right amount of nutrition. Here's what I mean: Over the past half century, levels of micronutrients (vitamins and minerals) in commercially grown produce have declined significantly. Biochemistry professor Donald Davis at the University of Texas in Austin published a landmark study showing a marked decline in several nutrients in today's produce.[5]

Corn and soy derivatives are added to almost all processed foods. This allows farmers to produce massive amounts of commodity crops without worrying about flooding the market, but it also contributes to our nutrient-deficient diets.

Many crops are harvested too early, before they can absorb necessary amounts of vitamins and minerals , like nitrogen (N), potassium (K), zinc (Zn), iron (Fe), magnesium (Mg), calcium (Ca), and more, from the soil.

Herbs, edible flowers, and flowering vegetables attract pollinators, confuse pests, and contain health-promoting polyphenols.

From 1950–1999, forty-three different fruits and vegetables declined in protein, calcium, phosphorus, iron, riboflavin, and vitamin C. Davis attributed these decreases to agricultural processes that have favored faster growth and pest resistance over nutrient density. "Efforts to breed

> "Poor soil health leads to poor plant health, which leads to poor human health."

new varieties of crops that provide greater yield, pest resistance, and climate adaptability have allowed crops to grow bigger and more rapidly, but their ability to manufacture or uptake nutrients has not kept pace with their rapid growth," Davis said in an interview with *Scientific American*.[6]

Davis's study was not alone in its findings. Similar studies conducted by The Kushi Institute and researcher D.E. Thomas observed similar decreases in levels of nutrients in today's commercially grown produce. Micronutrients like iron, sodium, potassium, magnesium, calcium, copper, and zinc were significantly lower in fruits and vegetables of today compared with produce from the 1940s–1970s.[7]

Thomas explains these findings as a by-product of the overuse of NPK (nitrogen, phosphorous, and potassium) fertilizers. These inorganic fertilizers raise concentrations of nitrogen, phosphorus, and potassium, while leaving the soil devoid of other critical nutrients. In contrast, manure, especially in solid form, improves soil pH, helps the earth absorb water, and is even more effective at increasing total nitrogen content.[8]

A plant unable to take up adequate nutrients from the soil produces fruit with less nutrition. Poor soil health leads to poor plant health, which leads to poor human health.

The Benefits of Growing Your Own Food

1. **It Improves Your Mental Health**
2. **It Promotes Physical Health**
3. **It Fosters Connection and Social Engagement**
4. **It Increases Self-Reliance**
5. **It Reduces Your Food Costs**

The advantages of starting a backyard garden go far beyond having access to nutritious food. Growing your own food has a holistic effect on your wellness—improving your mental, physical, and spiritual health. Sourcing food close to home is environmentally sustainable and dramatically reduces your carbon footprint. Gardening also fosters a sense of connection to friends and neighbors with whom you share your bounty and a deeper relationship to the earth that provides.

1. It Improves Your Mental Health

Gardening, known as "horticultural therapy" in the psychology community, improves memory, boosts mood, and reduces stress and anxiety. Cultivating plants is associated with improved physical and emotional well-being, sense of purpose, social inclusion, interpersonal relationships, and overall quality of life.[9] Working in a garden can effectively reduce anxiety after a stressful event[10] and improve symptoms of depression by increasing self-esteem.[11] Tending the soil has also been shown to improve addiction rehabilitation.[12, 13]

Horticultural therapy can even lower your risk of dementia by 36 percent.[14] A meta-analysis of over ten studies found that horticulture can be effectively used as a way to prevent cognitive decline.[15] One group of researchers found a possible explanation for some of these associations. Older adults who started a community garden tended to have less inflammation and fewer age-related changes to their immunity than non-gardeners. Growing plants helped participants feel younger and stronger.[16]

> "You can burn over 300 calories within an hour of gardening."

The everyday tasks of gardening (mulching, digging, weeding, etc.) are multipurpose. You're cultivating food for yourself and your family while also getting some much-recommended exercise.

2. It Promotes Physical Health

Spending time in the garden ameliorates the most common vitamin deficiency in America.[17] Just ten to thirty minutes per day most days of the week are enough to maintain healthy blood levels of vitamin D. Adequate levels of vitamin D are associated with decreased risk of several types of cancer, including breast, colorectal, and prostate cancer as well as non-Hodgkin's lymphoma.[18] In contrast, low vitamin D has been linked to psoriasis, metabolic syndrome, type 2 diabetes, and dementia. Digging in the earth has a multitude of health benefits that go far beyond absorbing vitamin D from sunshine.

If you've ever dug a decent-sized hole, you know gardening is exercise! You can burn over 300 calories within an hour of gardening. Pulling weeds, raking leaves, turning compost, transferring transplants . . . they're all considered "moderate

"If you're an athlete, plant-based foods are essential for reducing inflammation caused by intense workouts."

Just as plants require sunshine, so do we. Gardening is a great motivation for spending time outside and absorbing necessary vitamin D.

Simply touching the earth with your bare hands has been shown to relieve stress.

physical activity" by the Centers for Disease Control (CDC). And they recommend you should get at least thirty minutes of moderate activity most days of the week to maintain your weight and reduce your risk of disease.[19]

Edibles from the garden are high in nutrients and low in calories. By consuming nutrient-dense foods, you will turn off the body's hunger signal with fewer calories. Many plant-based foods are also high in

Growing your own plants from seed is both a meditative and a physical activity—many older adults have experienced the health benefits this provides.

fiber and will keep your body feeling fuller for longer periods of time.

Stress, toxins, pollution, and the foods we eat can cause inflammation which can lead to conditions like cancer, diabetes, and heart disease. Many plant-based foods are high in phytonutrients, antioxidants, and flavonoids that reduce inflammation in the body. If you're an athlete, plant-based foods are essential for reducing inflammation caused by intense workouts.

By eating more plant-based foods, you will be consuming more foods that have an alkalizing effect on the body. When we're stressed or eat certain animal-based foods our pH drops, and our blood becomes too acidic. Unfortunately, low blood pH can cause fatigue, kidney stones, and the loss of bone mass. Minerals found in plants are alkali-forming and help maintain a healthy blood pH.

Chlorophyll is a pigment that is responsible for giving plants their green color. Chlorophyll has many health benefits including its ability to increase red blood cell production. More red blood cells mean easier transport of oxygen into your cells, thereby increasing energy levels.

3. It Fosters Connection and Social Engagement

On a metaphysical level, we crave connection—to others, to our food, and to the Earth. Gardening strengthens those connections on physical and chemical levels.

Yogis and physicists alike use "grounding," a technique involving increased bodily contact with the earth. Touching the ground with your bare hands, feet, or skin produces an exchange of electrons between your body and planet Earth. This realigns your body's magnetic field with that of the Earth's. Your body is more able to combat the outside electric fields created in our modern environments (hello, computer, phone, microwave, and more). Grounding decreases stress and inflammation in the body, improves circulation, reduces pain, and improves sleep.[20]

Gardening makes us feel more connected to the earth, of course, but it also helps connect us with others—we can share the work along the way and then share the bounty after the harvest.

Maintaining a garden makes it much easier to add more vegetable-rich and plant-based foods to your diet.

> *"You'll get higher quality vegetables for a lower cost by growing them at home rather than buying them at the store."*

4. It Increases Self-Reliance

Living through the coronavirus pandemic of 2020 to the present has shown us how scary food insecurity can be. Disruptions in shipping, natural and manmade disasters, plus decreased food access depleted our food system, leaving bare shelves at the grocery store. Growing your own food offers a greater level of food security. To a greater extent, you are protected from economics, politics, or shipping challenges. Furthermore, it's literally in your backyard, ready at a moment's notice.

5. It Reduces Your Food Costs

Growing your own food is not only cost effective, but it can also substantially decrease your food budget. According to the National Gardening Association, a well-kept garden can produce half a pound of produce per square foot each season. For the average-size backyard garden (600 square feet), that's equivalent to 300 pounds of produce, worth about $600 that would otherwise be spent at the supermarket. That's 10 percent of what the average American household spends on food each year.

The average cost of a garden is $70. Seeds are affordable, especially when compared to the pounds of fruits and vegetables they can produce. A packet of 100 tomato seeds costing $2.19 can yield up to seventy-five tomato plants that produce ten to thirty pounds of tomatoes, worth about $35. That's a savings over ten times the initial investment.

Never underestimate the abundance your garden can offer. Kale, for example, is a plant that just keeps on giving.

Gardening will bring you year-round joy—from your cool winter preparations all the way through to next fall's harvest.

PRESERVING YOUR HARVEST

Congratulations! You've taken the first steps—grown your very own garden full of delectable goodies, perused the produce at the farmers market, or visited the fantastic local farm everyone raves about! Now you're probably wondering what exactly you should do with all that zucchini and kale, those many radishes and peppers, or the absolute abundance of TOMATOES now overflowing your kitchen! Not to worry, there are plenty of options to keep your harvest safe and stored for (absolutely delicious) year-round use.

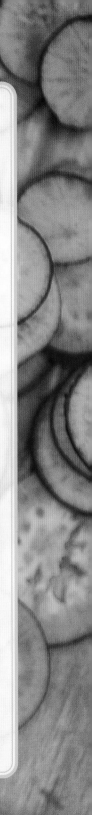

FREEZING

The easiest and most direct way to preserve your crops is likely staring you right in the face. Okay, maybe it's in the next room or garage or basement. I'm talking about your freezer.

There's a reason why freezers are so prevalent in modern kitchens. The convenience and ease of keeping food fresh in the freezer is as simple as: 1) dump food into a freezer-safe storage bag, 2) freeze for a reasonable amount of time, then 3) thaw and use.

Depending on the size of your garden and how ambitious you want to be in preserving it, consider investing in a chest or upright freezer. These vary in price and size, so pick the option that best suits your garden yield and storage needs.

Check out the tips that follow to make batch freezing an even more stress-free task.

Fruits

In general, freeze fruit in a freezer storage bag or plastic container for up to six to nine months. If you need a piece of fruit to maintain its shape or individuality—like stone fruits, berries, or bananas—first lay them in a single layer on a baking sheet and store them in the freezer for three hours. Then transfer them to a large freezable container, and repeat as necessary.

Thaw fruits in the fridge or on the counter. At room temperature, the high sugar content of fruit allows a quick thaw of only about a half an hour. Alternatively, fruits that will be used in muffins or cakes can be quickly added to prepared batter.

Vegetables and Herbs

Most vegetables can be tossed whole into a freezer bag and frozen as is. However, for best results, I recommend a quick blanch prior to freezing to maintain their flavor, nutrients, and shape. Here's how to do this:

1 **Clean and cut the vegetables into the desired sizes and shapes.** Then transfer them to a pot of boiling water and cook them submerged for 2 to 3 minutes.

2 **Transfer the vegetables to an ice-water bath.** Then transfer them to a colander or warming rack to let them cool and dry.

3 **Blot the vegetables with a paper towel to remove excess moisture.** Divide them into single-use portions before placing them in freezer bags or food storage containers. To slow freezer burn, make sure to remove as much air as possible from freezer bags, and fill food storage containers to the top. Double-bag pungent foods like onions and garlic to prevent aromas from permeating into other foods.

Stem tender herbs and place them in ice-cube trays filled with extra-virgin olive oil or water. Alternatively, leave hardier herbs like rosemary and thyme on their stems and freeze them in a freezer bag or food storage container.

Tips for Success: Dos and Don'ts of Freezing

Do:

1. Choose the best of the harvest for freezing, and thoroughly wash it prior to storage.
2. Label foods with their names and the dates they were placed in the freezer.
3. Use prepared frozen foods within three months. Store fruits and vegetables for 8 to 12 months in the freezer.
4. Keep the freezer at 0°F or below.

Don't:

1. Freeze foods in glass jars. Liquids expand as they freeze, and often cause poorly tempered glass to shatter in the freezer. If you are in a pinch and must freeze something in a glass jar, make sure to leave plenty of headspace (2 inches, to be on the safe side).
2. Thaw frozen foods using hot water. Thawing with hot water or a high microwave setting risks overcooking the food and compromising the texture and taste.
3. Disregard temperature danger zones. Allowing food to sit at room or refrigeration temperatures for too long allows exponential microbial growth in only a matter of hours. To avoid spoilage, chill food from 120°F to 70°F within 2 hours, and from 70°F to 45°F within 4 hours.

DRYING

The ideal pantry, or larder, is a dark, dry storage room with a consistent temperature between 50°F and 70°F and 60-percent humidity.^

Underground root cellars are the cooler cousin of a larder. To achieve maximum efficiency, root cellars should maintain temperatures between 32°F and 40°F, and have an 85- to 95-percent humidity. These were a mainstay of colonial life in the 1800s. They began to lose popularity with the invention of refrigeration, but they are making a comeback, as people increasingly garden and store food for longer periods.

Most vegetables decompose more slowly if their roots remain intact. This is particularly true for carrots, beets, and other root vegetables. On the other hand, leaves tend to perish quickly, so snip the tops of beets, radishes, carrots, and turnips prior to storing them in the pantry, refrigerator, or root cellar.

Most garden-fresh produce has a longer shelf life when stored unwashed. Some can even be left in the garden for weeks, as long as temperatures don't vary widely. Once produce is harvested, remove excess dirt and sand by gently shaking off visible dirt and wiping with a clean towel or paper towel. Wash produce thoroughly with tepid water immediately prior to consumption. Washing produce with cold water can cause foods to absorb surface pathogens more easily.*

Consider storing this produce in your larder (instead of your refrigerator) to prevent premature spoilage:

- Onions, garlic, and shallots
- Potatoes, sweet potatoes, and yams
- Nightshades such as tomatoes, cucumbers, and eggplants (up to 14 days)
- Tropical fruits such as bananas, avocadoes, mangos, papayas, pineapples, and kiwis
- Winter squash, such as pumpkins and butternut, spaghetti, acorn, and kabocha squashes

Some plants are best stored in standing water. Store asparagus, celery, and fresh herbs with their stems in a vase of clean water in a cool place in your kitchen.

^*Safe Home Food Storage. Texas Agrilife Extension Service by Peggy Van Laanen.*

Storing Garden Produce. The University of Maine. Cooperative Extension: Food and Health.

Three Ways to Preserve Food by Drying

Drying is the oldest form of food preservation. It simply requires removal of food's moisture without cooking it. Here are three ways to dry food, starting with the easiest and most affordable.

1. Dehydrating

The most common and practical method for dehydrating food is by using an electric dehydrator. A dehydrator retails for $40 to $50 and is widely available at home goods and grocery stores. This compact appliance has a built-in fan which circulates air in between pieces of fruit or vegetables (or whatever you're drying) to hasten the drying process. As an added bonus, most of a food's vitamins and minerals are retained during dehydration. Dried food is also shelf stable for six to twelve months.

Drying Herbs by the Bunch

Herbs are easily air-dried by hanging bunches upside down in a place that is cool, dry, and well ventilated. One idea is to tie herb bunches to a drying or laundry rack with twine. Alternatively, speed up the process by using a low temperature setting on your dehydrator. Roots of medicinal herbs, like ginseng and ginger, also do well when thinly sliced before being dried in the dehydrator.

2. Freeze-Drying

Freeze-drying is one of the most effective ways to store food for long-term use. Freeze-dried goods can last up to twenty-five years. It doesn't take a rocket scientist to see the benefit of that kind of longevity.

Here's how it works: Food is frozen to the point at which all the liquid in it turns to solid ice. Then, the atmospheric pressure around the food is lowered, allowing for sublimation, a process in which any solid turns into gas. Neato, huh?

Despite the impressive shelf life of freeze-dried foods, there are several disadvantages to consider. Freeze-dried foods take up about as much space as their fresh brethren, so you don't actually save much room in the pantry. Secondly, the texture and oftentimes the flavor of foods are altered in the process. Further still, commercial freeze-dryers are cost prohibitive for most people, averaging around $3,000 for a modest model. Freeze-drying is also time consuming, with each cycle taking up to twenty-four hours.

3. Sun-Drying

Sun-drying is an age-old process of drying food (you guessed it) in the sunshine. Sun-dried tomatoes, raisins, and figs are a few notable favorites from around the globe.

Sun-drying is only appropriate for fruits and should not be used for vegetables. Fruit has the magical ratio of acid and sugar that prevents spoilage despite heat and humidity. The best conditions to dry fruit in the sun are admittedly rare for most of us (okay, I see you Californians. And yes, I'm jealous). Optimal conditions include a temperature of at least 85°F (30°C), humidity of less than 60 percent, and a nice breeze.

Other methods of dehydrating food test the limits of practicality. Most climates are too cold or too humid to allow for sun-drying produce. Drying food in the oven at low temperatures can be very time consuming and cost ineffective (cooling a house with the oven door cracked for a few hours seems a little counterintuitive to most). And freeze-dried food seems best left to astrophysicists.

Preparing Fruits and Vegetables for Drying

Note that dried fruit lasts longer than dried vegetables, thanks to fruits' higher sugar and acid content. Let's talk process.

1. Choose seasonal, ripened produce. Selecting fruits or vegetables past their prime with bruising, softening, or browning will produce suboptimal results. Here's where I insist on purchasing organic produce if you've decided to apply chemicals to your garden: herbicides and pesticides only become more concentrated in dehydrated plants.

2. Clean and peel your produce first. Use a clean washcloth and veg wash to remove any dirt or grit. Remove skins that may toughen as they dehydrate.

3. Slice produce thinly. Aim for slices ¼ inch or thinner. I recommend using a mandoline or the slicing attachment of your food processor to ensure consistently sized slices.

4. Blanch or dip. Fruits and vegetables benefit from a last-minute treatment prior to being dried. Dip fruit in an acidic solution to prevent browning. To make such a solution, combine 4 cups of water with either ¼ cup lemon juice or 1 tablespoon of vinegar, and mix well. Blanching helps many vegetables maintain their color and texture during the drying process. To blanch, cook your vegetables in boiling water, then cool them off immediately in ice water prior to dehydrating (see the Storage and Preservation Chart on pages 28–32).

Easy Dehydrator Recipe: Fruit Leather

Fruit leather is a lovely, healthy snack that's easy to keep on hand to add a sweet pop to a child's packed lunch. It also helps to brighten up slow workday afternoons.

Makes 1 sheet pan, about 10 servings

Prep time: 20 minutes

Processing time: 8 hours

Ingredients
- 2 cups fresh or frozen fruit, washed, peeled, and stones removed
- 2 tablespoons lemon juice
- Applesauce, as needed

1 **Place the fruit and lemon juice in a blender or food processor.** Puree for 2 minutes, until the mixture is smooth and homogenous. If the slurry is thinner than the consistency of melted sherbet, add 1 cup of applesauce to thicken it.

2 **Line the trays of a dehydrator with nonstick aluminum foil or parchment paper.** Pour the slurry onto the lined trays, and level it out to a ¼-inch thickness using a spatula.

3 **Dry for 8 hours, or until the sheen of the leather dulls and the fruit leather is no longer sticky.** Store the fruit leather in a plastic bag with a zipper enclosure for up to 9 months.

CANNING

Canning food is a dying art. Today, most Americans have little to no experience canning, for a variety of possible reasons—they may fail to see its value, or they may lack access to freshly harvested produce, or they don't have the time.

I'm not going to lie. Canning can be time-intensive, hard work. But here's the good news: in this section, I'm sharing the simplest, most efficient, and most delicious canning recipes I know. It's going to be so satisfying to open that jar of stewed tomatoes in December, or a jar of crunchy pickled radishes in mid-July.

For Safety's Sake: Three Canning Rules to Live By

- **Get a clean start.** Make sure to clean and sanitize jars, lids, rings, counter, and yes, even the kitchen sink before canning. (For instructions on how to sanitize jars, lids, and rings, see step 1 under "Water-Bath Canning for Acidic Foods" on the left.) Make sure your hands have been washed for at least 30 seconds prior to handling foods.
- **Drop the pH.** The more acidic the food, the less likely botulism will grow. This is especially true for foods with a pH of 4.6 or lower. Translation: don't skimp on the vinegar.
- **When in doubt, toss it out!** Any unsealed jars, or canned food with mold, an off smell, or questionable color should be discarded.

Canning equipment you'll need

- 18–21-quart water bath canner (canning pot) or pressure-canner*
- Canning jars
- Canning lids
- Jar rings/bands
- Jar lifter
- Wide-mouth funnel
- Spatula or wooden skewer

Other basic kitchen utensils and tools you'll need include knives, measuring cups and spoons, cooking spoons, a ladle, a potholder, a kitchen towel or paper towels, a timer, cutting boards, a candy thermometer, a vegetable peeler, pots, a saucepan, and mixing bowls.

Pressure canners are preferred only with lower acidity foods, like meats

> *"Canning requires an investment of time and hard work, but it all results in convenient, affordable, healthy vegetables you can enjoy year-round."*

What's better, canning offers several advantages to the home gardener. Have you considered the following?

1. Canning preserves nutrients. In fact, produce fresh from your garden that's processed quickly is significantly more nutrient dense than fruits and vegetables on a grocery store shelf. Fruits and vegetables lose only 5 to 20 percent of water-soluble vitamins when canned. This is less than half the nutrient loss when vegetables are stored in a warehouse, shipped long distances, and placed on grocery store shelves—a system that leads to a loss of more than 50 percent of some vitamins. Canning your own produce is a heck of a lot more environmentally friendly, too.

2. Canned foods are convenient. Once the work is done, you'll have a veritable feast at your fingertips. You can enjoy your favorite seasonal foods year-round. Plus, it makes meal prep a cinch when you're in a time crunch.

3. You can trust your canned foods. You have complete control of your food, and you know EXACTLY what's in it. No BPA-coated cans, no excess salt or preservatives, just homemade goodness.

4. Canned foods are affordable. Foods canned at home are less expensive and are impervious to food shortages and rising food costs.

5. Canning is fun. Dare I say it?! If you enjoy spending time in the kitchen, or better yet, seeing the smiles and health that your food brings, you just might enjoy canning. Reflecting over a batch of canned goods you grew in your own garden can be a source of joy and accomplishment.

There are two preferred methods of canning: water bath and pressure canning.

Additives (optional)

- **Vitamin C** is a helpful and healthful preservative when canning fruit, and it also helps to retain the colors of mushrooms and potatoes. A good rule of thumb is to add 3 grams of ascorbic acid (vitamin C) to 1 gallon of water.
- **Pectin** is a polysaccharide that helps jellies and jams set. Pectin combines with the natural sugars in the fruit to form a gel. This allows fruits without a lot of natural pectin (berries, for example) to thicken without having to add extra sugar. Add liquid pectin at the end of the cooking process. Powdered pectin is added to the fruit prior to adding sugar, according to the package instructions.

Water-Bath Canning Steps for Acidic Foods

1 Prep your jars. Prepare clean jars that have been thoroughly washed and rinsed by immersing them in hot water (140°F for raw/cold-packing and 180°F for hot-packing). This tempers the jars, so they don't crack when filled with hot liquid. Jars for foods processed for less than 10 minutes should be sanitized. To do this, heat the jars in boiling water at least 1 to 2 inches above their rims for 10 minutes. Jars and rings should be kept submerged in hot water until they are ready to be filled.

2 Prep your fruit or vegetables. Choose only the freshest produce, preferably harvested within the previous 24 hours. Peel away tough skins and stems, clean the fruit or vegetables well, and chop

Water-bath Canner

1–2 in. Airspace

1–2 in. Water

Rack

Pressure Canner

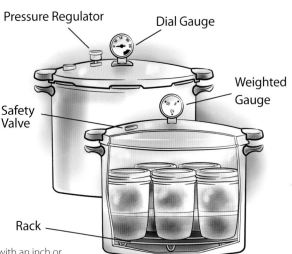

Pressure Regulator

Dial Gauge

Safety Valve

Weighted Gauge

Rack

Water-bath canners (left) are deep enough that you can cover the jars with an inch or two of water while still allowing boiling room above. Pressure canners (right) come in two basic styles: dial gauge and weighted gauge. Make sure all of the parts are in good working order.

them into the desired size and shape. If necessary, dip fruit into an acidic solution.

3a **Raw/cold-pack.** Pack unheated, raw produce into hot jars, then fill the jars with boiling liquid. This is often used for vegetables that will be pressure-canned.

3b **Hot-pack.** Place produce that has been boiled then simmered for 2 to 5 minutes into prepared jars. Hot-packing is often the preferred method for water-bath canning, as it is more effective at removing air. This ensures better color and flavor in the finished product. This method also requires fewer jars.

4 **Remove the air.** Remove air from canned goods by inserting a plastic spatula or wooden skewer between the food and the side of the jar. Move the spatula up and down while turning the jar to release any air bubbles.

5 **Add headspace.** Measure the distance between the top of the food and the top of the jar, adjusting as necessary to achieve the recommended headspace. Use a damp paper towel to clean the rim of the jar prior to topping it with the lid.

6 **Process filled jars.** Process jars immediately after packing them. Place the jars on the canning rack situated at the bottom of the canner. For a water bath, the water level should be 1 to 2 inches above the jars' rims. Start the timer once the water starts to boil. Reduce heat to maintain a gentle boil for the time indicated in the recipe. Add boiling water if necessary to keep the jars covered. Turn off the heat, remove the lid from the canner, and let the jars sit in hot water an additional 5 minutes before taking them out to cool.

7 **Cool the jars.** Line the countertop with folded towels. Remove the jars from the canner with a jar lifter and transfer them to the towels, allowing 1 to 2 inches of space between them. (To prevent improper sealing, make sure not to tip or invert the jars while removing them from the canner.) Listen for the sound of the lid—a high-pitched pop as it seals signals that a vacuum has been successfully created. Any jars that did not seal adequately can be processed again with a new lid. Leave all the jars to cool to room temperature, 12 to 24 hours. Discard food from any jars that have not sealed within 24 hours.

Pressure-Canning Steps for Low-Acid Foods

1 **Prep your jars.** Prepare clean jars that have been thoroughly washed and rinsed by immersing them in hot water (140°F for raw/cold packing and 180°F for hot packing). This tempers the jars, so they don't crack when filled with hot liquid. Jars for foods processed for less than 10 minutes should be sanitized. To do this, heat the jars in boiling water at least 1 to 2 inches above their rims for 10 minutes. Jars and rings should be kept submerged in hot water until they are ready to be filled.

2 **Prep your fruit or vegetables.** Peel away tough skins and stems, clean the fruit or vegetables well, and chop them into the desired size and shape.

3a **Raw/cold-pack.** Pack unheated, raw produce into hot jars, then fill the jars with boiling liquid. This is often used for vegetables that will be pressure-canned.

3b **Hot-pack.** Place produce that has been boiled then simmered for 2 to 5 minutes into prepared jars.

4 **Remove the air.** Remove air from canned goods by inserting a plastic spatula or wooden skewer between the food and the side of the jar. Move the spatula up and down while turning the jar to release any air bubbles.

5 **Add headspace.** Measure the distance between the top of the food and the top of the jar, adjusting as necessary to achieve the recommended headspace (1 to 1¼ inches for low-acid vegetables). Use a damp paper towel to clean the rim of the jar prior to topping it with the lid.

6 **Process filled jars.** Process jars immediately after packing. Fill the pressure canner with 2 inches of water and place the canner over high heat until the water begins to simmer. In a separate pot, boil additional water, to add in the

More Rules to Can By

Do:

1. Can fruits and vegetables at the peak of ripeness, preferably within 6 to 12 hours of harvest.
2. Use new lids every time to ensure a good seal.
3. Leave adequate headspace according to recipe instructions, to ensure proper sealing.
4. Use canning or pickling salt to ensure consistency and a clear brine.
5. Maintain water at a rolling boil and cover the jars with at least 1 inch of water above the rim when processing them in a water bath.
6. Have the dial pressure gauge on your canner tested annually.
7. Test the seal of processed jars using one of three methods:
   a) Press the middle of the lid down with a finger. If the lid springs back up, the jar is not sealed.
   b) Tap the lid with a metal spoon. If the lid makes a high-pitched "ping," the jar is sealed. Unsealed jars make a dull sound. (Note: food touching the bottom of the lid can also produce a dull sound.)
   c) Look for a shallow, concave depression in the center of the lid. Its presence indicates that the jar is sealed.

Don't:

1. Settle for bruised, under-ripened produce, or fruits and vegetables that are past their prime.
2. Leave cut fruit and vegetables exposed to air for long periods of time prior to canning.
3. Use jars with glass or zinc lids (they almost never seal properly).
4. Can using an open kettle, microwave, conventional oven, or dishwasher. These methods are inconsistent at best and dangerous at worst.
5. Taste-test jars of food that have mold, an off odor, bulging lids, or are leaking. These are all signs of food spoilage. Toss the contents out.

canning process as needed. Place the jars on the canning rack situated at the bottom of the canner. Fasten the lid and let steam escape from the open petcock or weighted gauge opening for 10 minutes. Close the petcock or put on the weighted gauge to increase the pressure. Once the pressure has reached 10 pounds (or as specified in the recipe), reduce the heat to medium low and start the timer. Process for the time specified in the recipe, making sure the pressure is maintained by increasing or decreasing the heat with any fall or rise in pressure, respectively. Remove the canner from heat. Let the pressure return to 0 (about 2 minutes) before opening the lid away from you.

7 Cool the jars. Line the countertop with folded towels. Remove the jars from the canner with a jar lifter and transfer them to the towels, allowing 1 to 2 inches of space between them. (To prevent improper sealing, make sure not to tip or invert the jars while removing them from the canner.) Listen for the sound of the lid—a high-pitched pop as it seals signals that a vacuum has been successfully created. Any jars that did not seal adequately can be processed again with a new lid. Leave all the jars to cool to room temperature, 12 to 24 hours. Discard food from any jars that have not sealed within 24 hours.

Troubleshooting

Mold on top: Toss it. Conventional wisdom held that a jam or canned vegetable could be salvaged by scraping off the mold on top. We now know that mycotoxins, a byproduct of mold or fungi, can cause serious illness or even death. Spores that are inhaled can also be dangerous, so throw away unopened jars that have any sign of spoilage.

Poorly sealed jars: Try again. Jars that are not properly sealed can be reprocessed if discovered within 24 hours. Remove the lid of a poorly sealed jar and inspect for chips or cracks in the jar by carefully running your finger around the opening of the jar. Transfer the contents to a new jar if needed and cover with a new, sanitized lid. Process again using the original processing time.

Cloudy liquid or sediments in jars: Learn and adjust for next time. Rarely a sign of spoilage, these conditions often result from using table salt or water with a high mineral content. To prevent this in the future, choose produce that has not passed its peak of ripeness, use soft or distilled water, and use canning or pickling salt.

Easy Steps to Take to Avoid Spoilage

1 Use a cool, dry storage space. To prevent spoilage, store canned goods in a cool, dry place and use within 12 months. Canned goods exposed to sunlight or temperatures over 95°F (35°C) are more likely to have microbial growth and spoil. Lids stored in high humidity can rust, increasing the probability of contamination.

2 Ensure adequate headspace. Foods without enough headspace are also prone to spoilage. This is because the food can expand and break the seal, allowing microbes to be introduced into the jar. Highly acidic foods, such as pickled or fermented goods, can eat away at the lid, giving microbes an entrance opportunity.

3 Clean and stem produce. Using produce that has not been adequately washed or has stems intact can lead to a high microbial load inside the jar. Rinse and rub nightshades, root vegetables, and fruits for five seconds to remove dirt or girt. Perform a final rinse before peeling or chopping.

4 Go the extra mile. Soak leafy greens, cruciferous (certain brassicas) vegetables, artichokes, celery, and fennel in a slightly acidic solution for 2 minutes, then rinse with water for an additional 15 seconds prior to use. To prepare the acidic soaking solution, use a ratio of ¼ cup white vinegar or lemon juice for each 1 cup of water.

Storage and Preservation Chart

	Water-Bath Canning	Pressure-Canning (at 10 pounds pressure)
Apples	• Pint: 20 min • Quart: 20 min • Hot: Peel, core and segment, cover with water and 1 teaspoon lemon juice and boil for 5 min; leave ½ inch headspace	Appropriate for water bath canning
Asparagus	Not recommended (low acid vegetable)	• Pint: 30 min • Quart: 40 min • Raw pack: ½ inch headspace • Hot pack: Boil for 2 minutes; ½ inch headspace
Wax/String Beans	Not recommended (low acid vegetable)	• Pint: 20 min • Quart: 25 min • Raw: ½-inch headspace • Hot: Boil 5 minutes; ½-inch headspace
Beets and other roots (e.g. Radishes, Parsnips, and Turnips)	Not recommended (low acid vegetable)	• Pint: 30 min • Quart: 35 min • Hot: Boil for 15 minutes and peel; 1-inch headspace
Berries	• Pint: 15 min • Quart: 15 min • Hot: Add ¼ cup honey or water per pint of berries and bring to a boil; ½-inch headspace	Appropriate for water bath canning
Broccoli	Not recommended (low acid vegetable)	Not recommended
Brussels sprouts	Not recommended (low acid vegetable)	Not recommended
Cabbage	Not recommended (low acid vegetable)	Not recommended
Carrots	Not recommended (low acid vegetable)	• Pint: 25 min • Quart: 30 min • Raw: wash well and pack tightly; 1-inch headspace • Hot: bring to a boil; ½-inch headspace
Celery	Not recommended (low acid vegetable)	Not recommended
Corn	Not recommended (low acid vegetable)	• Pint: 55 min • Quart: 85 min • Hot: Add 1 cup water to corn kernels and boil for 5 minutes; pack loosely; 1-inch headspace

Freezing	Dehydrating	Storage
Peel, core, slice, and dip into 1 quart of water with three 500 mg vitamin C tablets dissolved into it.	Core and cut into ½-inch rings and pre-treat with acidic solution prior to drying. Shelf-life: 6 months at room temp.	• Dry/Refrigerated: Store at 32°F for up to 6 months. • Frozen: 8 months • Canned: 18 months
Trim tough ends and blanch 2-4 minutes until crisp tender, then transfer to freezer bag.	Use only the top 3 inches. Boil or steam for 5 minutes prior to drying. Shelf-life: 2 months at room temp.	• Refrigerator: 2 weeks; place stems in a glass of water; refresh water every 2-3 days • Frozen: 1 year • Canned: 2-5 years
Wash, trim ends, and blanch for 3 minutes, then transfer to freezer bag.	Cook beans for 30 minutes at 160°F. Shelf-life: 4 months at room temp.	• Refrigerator: 7 days • Frozen: 1 year • Canned: 2-5 years
Wash, remove tops and roots. Roast at 375°F until fork tender. Let cool and transfer to a freezer bag.	Remove tops and roots and boil for 30-45 minutes, until tender before drying. Shelf-life: 4 months at room temp.	• Refrigerated: 4-6 months; remove greens and store unwashed • Frozen: 1 year • Canned: 2-5 years
Destem, wash, and dry berries. Freeze whole on a baking sheet then transfer to freezer bag.	Stem and cut berries larger than 1 inch in diameter in half before drying. Pretreat with acidic solution. Shelf-life: 6 months at room temp.	• Refrigerated: 5 days; unwashed, cover loosely in a single layer • Frozen: 8 months • Canned: 18 months
Wash, remove leaves and tough stem, and separate into florets. Blanch for 3-5 minutes and store in a freezer bag.	Remove the stalk and slice into ½-inch strips. Steam for 5 minutes prior to drying. Shelf-life: 1 month at room temp.	• Spritz broccoli with water and wrap in a damp paper towel prior to storing in the crisper drawer for 1-2 weeks
Blanch for 3-5 minutes and store in a freezer bag.	Not recommended	• Leave Brussels sprouts in the garden until early January
Blanch clean leaves for 90 seconds and store in freezer bags.	Cut into ½-inch slices. Steam for 4 minutes before drying. Shelf-life: 1 month at room temp.	• Refrigerated: 1-6 months; remove outer leaves • Extend shelf-life by fermenting.
Peel, slice, cube, or leave whole. Blanch for 2-5 minutes depending on size. Freeze on a baking sheet and transfer to a freezer bag.	Slice cleaned carrots into ½-inch slices. Boil for 4 minutes before drying. Shelf-life: 6 months at room temp.	• Refrigerated: 7-9 months • Frozen: 1 year • Canned: 2-5 years
Wash, remove leaves, and dice and freeze on a baking sheet then transfer to a freezer bag.	Slice into ¼-inch pieces. Steam for 4 minutes before drying. Shelf-life: 2 months at room temp.	• Refrigerated: 2-3 months when stems are in fresh water • Frozen: 1 year
Shuck, remove silk, cut off ends, and blanch for 6 minutes prior to cutting off kernels or transferring whole cob to freezer bag.	Remove the husk and silk. Boil whole cob for 4 minutes. Remove kernels from the cob before drying. Shelf-life: 4 months at room temp.	• Refrigerated: 3 days; store in a plastic bag to keep moist • Frozen: 1 year • Canned: 2-5 years

	Water-Bath Canning	Pressure-Canning (at 10 pounds pressure)
Figs	• Pint: 45 min • Quart: 50 min • Hot: Cover with water and boil for 5 min; add 1 tablespoon lemon juice for each pint; ½-inch headspace	• Pint: 10 min at 5 pounds pressure if no acid is added
Garlic	Not recommended (low acid vegetable)	• Pint: 30 min • Quart: 40 min • Boil water then remove from heat. Cook garlic for 10 min in hot water; ½-inch headspace
Grapes	• Pint: 15 min • Quart: 20 min • Raw: Wash, stem, pack tightly, and cover with boiling water; ½-inch headspace	Appropriate for water bath canning
Herbs	Not recommended	Not recommended
Onion	Not recommended (low acid vegetable)	• Pint: 25 min • Quart: 30 min • Hot: Boil for 5 min; pack loosely; ½-inch headspace
Oranges, grapefruits, tangerines	• Pint: 10 min • Quart: 10 min • Raw: Peel, seed, and segment, removing all with pith and membranes; ½-inch headspace	Appropriate for water bath canning
Peas	Not recommended (low acid vegetable)	With pods: • Pint: 20 min • Quart: 25 min • Raw: Pack loosely; 1-inch headspace Shelled: • Pint: 40 min • Quart: 40 min • Raw/Hot: pack loosely; 1-inch headspace
Pears	• Pint: 20 min • Quart: 25 min • Hot: Peel, halve, and core. Add 1 teaspoon lemon juice and enough water to cover and heat to boil; ½-inch headspace	Appropriate for water bath canning

Freezing	Dehydrating	Storage
Wash, stem, and squeeze lemon juice on whole figs prior to freezing on a baking sheet, then transfer to a freezer bag.	Cut in half before drying. Pretreat with acidic solution before drying.	• Dry storage: 3 days • Refrigerated: 1 week • Frozen: 8 months • Canned: up to 2 years
Freeze whole cloves unpeeled or chopped garlic in a freezer bag.	Peel and cut into thin pieces. Shelf-life: 4 months at room temp.	• Dry storage: 6-7 months in a at 40°F; store in a garlic braid by wrapping and tying the garlic stems with twine • Refrigerated: 3 months when packed in oil • Frozen: 8 months • Canned: 2-5 years
Wash, stem, and freeze on a baking sheet then transfer to a freezer bag.	Use only seedless grapes. Cut an x into the skins of the grapes, then blanch for 1 minute and peel before drying.	• Dry storage: Store at 32°F for up to 2 months. • Frozen: 8 months • Canned: 18 months
Freeze leaves in an ice cube tray filled with olive oil or water.	• Dry leaves at 95-115°F in the dehydrator, or air dry by hanging upside down in a low-humidity environment. • Place dried plants with seeds like coriander or dill in a paper bag and shake vigorously to release the seeds.	• Store in the garden until ready for use. Protect parsley from hot summers and cold winters by adding up to 2 feet of mulch. Once cut, place stems in a vase of water. • Frozen: 8 months
Peel, slice, or dice and store in a freezer bag.	Peel and slice onions. Blanch for 4 minutes. Shelf-life: 4 months at room temp.	• Dry Storage: Hang onions for 6-7 months at (33-45°F) in old stockings by tying a knot in between each onion. Cut the stocking right above the lowest onion when ready to use. • Frozen: 8 months • Canned: 2-5 years
Peel, seed, and segment, removing all with pith and membranes and store in a freezer bag.	Dry citrus zest on a cheesecloth covered rack in the dehydrator for 1-2 hours.	• Refrigerated: up to 8 weeks • Frozen: 12 months • Canned: 18 months
• With pods: wash, trim and remove strings and blanch for 2 minutes, then transfer to a freezer bag • Shelled: Blanch in boiling water for 2 minutes and store in freezer bag	Shell peas and blanch for 5 minutes prior to drying. Shelf-life: 4 months at room temp.	• Dry Storage: Store dried peas in an airtight bag or jar indefinitely. Discard if moldy. • Refrigerated: 7 days • Canned: 2-5 years
Not recommended	Slice into ½-inch rings and treat with acidic solution prior to drying.	• Dry Storage: Store 1-3 months in a cool, dry place. Ripen at room temp. • Refrigerated: 5-10 days • Canned: 18 months

	Water-Bath Canning	Pressure-Canning (at 10 pounds pressure)
Peppers	Not recommended (low acid vegetable)	• Pint: 35 min • Hot: Peel peppers prior to canning; ½-inch headspace
Potatoes	Not recommended (low acid vegetable)	• Pint: 35 min • Quart: 40 min • Hot: Peel and cube or leave smaller potatoes whole. Use 1 teaspoon salt in 1 quart water to prevent browning; 1-inch headspace
Pumpkins and winter squash	Not recommended (low acid vegetable)	• Pint: 55 min • Quart: 90 min • Hot: Seed, peel, and cube, then boil for 2 minutes; 1-inch headspace
Spinach and other greens (e.g. Kale, Beet, Turnip, Mustard, and Chard)	Not recommended (low acid vegetable)	• Pint: 70 min • Quart: 90 min • Hot: Remove tough stems and ribs; steam for 10 min; 1-inch headspace
Stone fruit	• Pint: 20 min • Quart: 25 min • Raw: Prick skins prior to covering with boiling water • Hot: Prick skin, cover with water and 1 teaspoon lemon juice and boil; leave ½-inch headspace	Appropriate for water bath canning
Sweet Potatoes	Not recommended	• Pint: 65 min • Quart: 90 min • Hot: Peel and cube then boil for 20 minutes; leave 1-inch headspace
Tomatoes	• Pint: 40 min • Quart: 45 min • Hot: Score the tomatoes into 4 segments, then blanch to remove the skins then bring to a boil. Add 4 teaspoons lemon juice or ½ teaspoons citric acid for every quart of tomatoes; leave 1-inch headspace	Appropriate for water bath canning
Zucchini and summer squash	Not recommended	Not recommended

Freezing	Dehydrating	Storage
Freeze whole, sliced, or diced. Blister skins under a broiler to ease removal, if desired.	Create a pepper garland by threading a needle through the thickest part of the pepper. Hang to dry in a low-humidity environment. Shelf-life: 8 months at room temp.	• Dry Storage: Store dried peppers in an airtight container for up to two years. • Refrigerated: 1-2 weeks • Frozen: 8-12 months • Canned: 2-5 years
Cube waxy potatoes and freeze on a baking sheet, then transfer to a freezer bag.	Slice into ½-inch rounds and steam for 8 minutes prior to drying. Shelf-life: 4 months at room temp.	• Dry storage/refrigerated: Store in a root cellar or refrigerator at 40°F for up to 6 months. • Frozen: up to 1 year • Canned: 2-5 years
Roast at 375°F until fork tender. Scoop flesh from skin and store in a freezer bag.	Clean squash, then cut into segments, roast at 350°F for 45-50 minutes until tender before drying. Shelf-life: 1 month at room temp,	• Dry storage: Harvest once the squash skin is hardened and store in a cool, dark place at 50-60°F for up to six months • Frozen: 8-12 months • Canned: 2-5 years
Blanch for 2 minutes before transferring to a freezer storage bag.	De-stem tough varieties and tear into 2-inch pieces. Dehydrate at 125°F for 2 hours in the dehydrator, or 30 minutes at 225°F in the oven.	• Refrigerated: 5 days; wash, dry and wrap in paper towels. • Frozen: 8 months • Canned: 2-5 years
Freeze whole in large freezer bags. To use, slice while still frozen or loosen skins by pouring boiling water over frozen peaches, nectarines, or plums.	Pit and cut into thin slices. Pretreat with acidic solution before drying. Shelf-life: 8 months at room temp.	• Dry Storage: Ripen at room temperature. Keep away from foods that are susceptible to ethylene gas • Refrigerated: 5 days after ripening • Frozen: 8 months • Canned: 18 months
Peel and slice into rings or cubes. Cook until tender. Mash if desired. Pack in freezer bags and freeze on a flat surface up to 8-12 months.	Wash well, cut into ½-inch rounds, steam for 8 minutes before drying. Shelf-life: 1 month at room temp.	• Dry storage: up to 6 months at 40°F • Frozen: 8-12 months • Canned: 1 year
Freeze whole tomatoes on a baking sheet, then transfer to a freezer bag.	Halve smaller tomatoes, cut large tomatoes into thirds, prior to blanching for 2 minutes to remove skins prior to drying at 120°F for 24 hours. Store tomatoes in a jar covered with olive oil for up to 1 month in the refrigerator.	• Dry storage: 1 week; store tomatoes at 50-60°F one layer deep in a shallow tray • Frozen: 8 months • Canned: 18 months
Quickly blanch, then slice or shred prior to storing in a freezer bag.	Slice into thin strips and blanch for 4 minutes before drying. Shelf-life: 1 month at room temp.	• Refrigerated: 1 week; leave whole • Frozen: 8 months • Canned: 2 years

Canning Recipes

Canning the best of your produce enables you to enjoy your harvest all year long. I've included my favorite canning recipes—flavorful, uncomplicated, and fool-proof. While I often encourage experimentation and putting your own spin on recipes, I recommend sticking to these recipes without deviation. Cutting back on the acidity or salt or increasing the substrate can promote bacterial growth and become a health hazard. And remember, when in doubt, throw it out.

Master Vegetable Brine Recipe

I am an acidophile. I love adding vinegar or citrus to a dish to give it that bright note of acidity. This pickling brine has a mild flavor to accentuate any veggie harvested from your garden.

Makes: 3 quarts • **Prep time:** 2 mins. • **Cook time:** 5–7 mins.

Ingredients

- ½ cup white vinegar
- ½ cup rice wine vinegar
- 3 cups water
- ½ cup granulated sugar
- 3 tablespoons canning/pickling salt

1. Place all ingredients in a large pot over high heat. Whisk the solution until the solids have dissolved and the mixture has come to a boil.
2. Pour the hot brine over the vegetables in each jar, leaving 1 inch of headspace. Process as recommended in the Storage and Preservation Chart (see pages 28–32).

Canned Fruit Master Recipe

This fruit syrup has the same sugar content as that of most fruits, mimicking fruit juice without having to do the extra work of extracting the juice. This syrup helps whole and halved fruits retain their color, flavor, and shape.

Makes: 9 pints • **Prep time:** Varies by fruit • **Cook time:** 5–7 minutes

Ingredients
- 6½ cups water
- ¼ cup honey
- ½ cup granulated sugar

1. Place all ingredients in a large pot over high heat. Whisk the solution frequently until the solids have dissolved and the mixture has come to a boil.
2. Add the fruit and bring the mixture back to a boil. Pour the hot fruit into prepared jars and process as recommended in the Storage and Preservation Chart (see pages 28–32).

Quick Pickles

Can you pickle any cucumber? Absolutely. Are pickling cucumbers better for pickling? Absolutely. Slicing cucumbers are also better eaten fresh, but I encourage you not to limit yourself if you have 20 pounds of cucumbers decomposing on your countertop as you read this. Pickling cucumbers have thinner skins and drier flesh that can more easily absorb pickling brine without losing turgor. Minimize softening during fermentation by cutting off the blossom end of the cucumber.

Makes: 4 quarts • **Prep time:** 25 mins. • **Cook time:** 7 mins. • **Processing time:** 15 mins.

Ingredients

- 2 pounds pickling cucumbers, such as Kirby, Boston Pickling, English Hothouse, Parisian, Homemade Pickles, Pick a Bushel or Supremo
- ¾ cup distilled white vinegar
- ½ cup apple cider vinegar
- ⅓ cup granulated sugar
- ¼ cup kosher salt
- 6 garlic cloves, peeled and left whole
- 1 bunch fresh dill, separated into sprigs
- 1½ teaspoons whole peppercorns
- 1½ teaspoons mustard seeds

1. Slice, spear, or leave the cucumbers whole, as desired. In a medium saucepan, heat the vinegars, sugar, and salt over medium heat. Stir the solution and remove it from heat once the sugar and salt have dissolved.
2. Distribute the cucumbers, garlic, dill, peppercorns, and mustard seeds equally among quart jars. Cover them with the vinegar solution, leaving a 1-inch headspace at the top of each jar, and seal the jars with lids.
3. Refrigerate the pickles for up to 3 months, or process them for 15 minutes (at 0–1,000 feet altitude) in a boiling water bath. Refrigerate after opening.

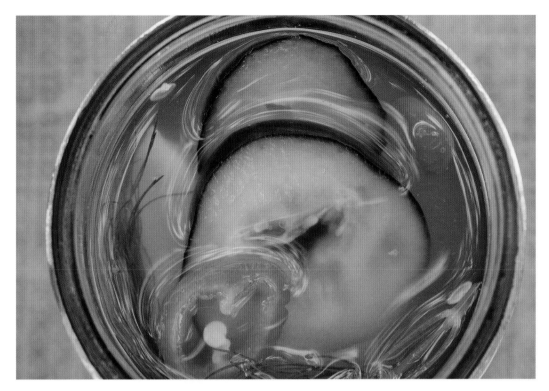

Refrigerator Sweet and Spicy Pickles

I've tried many, *many* pickle recipes. Lightly sweet with a garlicky kick and easy enough to throw together in a moment's notice, this is the recipe I always come back to.

Makes: 3 quarts • **Prep time:** 3 mins. • **Cook time:** 3 mins. • **Inactive prep time:** 6+ hrs.

Ingredients

- 8 pickling cucumbers, sliced
- 1 jalapeño, sliced
- 3 cloves garlic, peeled and smashed
- 3 sprigs fresh dill
- 2 cups white vinegar
- 1 cup apple cider vinegar
- ½ cup sugar
- 2 tablespoons salt

1. Divide the sliced cucumbers, jalapeño slices, garlic, and dill equally among three 1-quart mason jars.
2. Combine the vinegars, sugar, and salt in a pot and cook on medium heat, stirring occasionally. Bring it to a slow boil and remove it from heat.
3. Pour the vinegar mixture over the ingredients in jars, and place the jars in the refrigerator. Let them pickle for at least 6 hours. They can be stored in the refrigerator for up to 2 months.

Pickled Okra

Pickled okra is a staple of the South. Customize your preserved okra by adding banana or chile peppers, mustard seeds, fresh dill, or the last of summer's tomatoes. Enjoy pickled okra on salads or on a crudité platter.

Makes: 3 pints • **Prep time:** 10 mins. • **Cook time:** 5 mins. • **Processing time:** 25 mins.

Ingredients

- 1 pound okra, washed, with stems removed
- 3 cloves garlic
- 1 teaspoon peppercorns
- 1½ teaspoons dill seeds
- 1½ tablespoons canning salt
- ½ teaspoon sugar
- 1½ cups water
- ½ cup rice wine vinegar

1. Divide the okra, garlic, peppercorns, and dill seeds equally among jars.
2. Place a small pot containing the salt, sugar, water, and vinegar over high heat. Stir the mixture until the solids dissolve and the liquid is boiling.
3. Pour the liquid over the okra in the jars, leaving 1 inch of headspace. Seal and process the jars for 25 minutes in a boiling water bath. Refrigerate after opening.

Rickles (Pickled Radishes)

When you get really good at gardening (and believe me, you'll get there), you're going to have a glut of vegetables that you may or may not have a plan for. Rickles came out of my desperation to preserve a sizable pile of radishes in a pinch. These days we plant too many radish seeds just so I can make them. They are *that* good.

Makes: 1 pint • **Prep time:** 7 mins. • **Cook time:** 7 mins. • **Processing time:** 10 mins.

Ingredients

- ½ pound radishes, washed, with ends removed
- 2 cloves garlic
- 2 sprigs fresh dill
- 1 teaspoon mustard seeds
- 3 black peppercorns
- ½ cup sugar
- 1 teaspoon salt
- ¾ cup white vinegar

1. Slice the radishes into ½-inch rounds. Pack the radish slices, garlic, dill, mustard seeds, and peppercorns tightly into a sterilized pint jar.
2. Stir the sugar and salt into the vinegar in a medium saucepan over high heat. Bring it to a boil.
3. Pour the hot liquid into the jar, leaving ½ inch of headspace. Seal and process the jar for 10 minutes in a boiling water bath for long-term storage, or refrigerate it for up to 2 months.

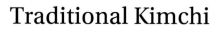

Traditional Kimchi

You've probably heard of Korean kimchi, fermented cabbage robust with heat and gut-restoring probiotics. This condiment lives up to the hype with layers of flavor and texture—sour, spicy, tangy, and crunchy. Though traditionally made with Napa cabbage, kimchi can be made with any variety of cabbage (red cabbages make a lovely purple kimchi, by the way). Bok or pak choy are also good stand-ins. Gochugaru (GO-choo-GAH-roo), a red chili pepper spice with smoky, fruity notes, has no substitute. Find gochugaru in the spices or Asian section of most large grocers, or with a quick online search.

Makes: 2 quarts • **Prep time:** 30 mins. • **Inactive prep time:** 2–5 days • **Processing time:** 15 mins.

Ingredients

- 1 head (2–3 pounds) cabbage, cut into 1-inch chunks
- ½ cup salt
- ½ pound radishes, cut into matchsticks
- 4 carrots, peeled and cut into matchsticks
- ¼ cup gochugaru
- 1 bunch (4–6) scallions, cut into 1-inch pieces
- 2 tablespoons garlic, minced
- 1 tablespoon fresh ginger, grated
- 1 teaspoon sugar

1. Wash the cabbage well and place it in a large bowl. Add salt and enough water to submerge the cabbage. Let it sit for 1–2 hours.
2. Rinse the cabbage and place it in a colander to drain. Return the cabbage to the bowl and add the remaining ingredients. Stir well until all ingredients are well incorporated. Spoon the mixture into clean, sterilized canning jars and pack the kimchi down to remove air.
3. Place lids on the jars and store them in a cool (70°F–75°F), dry place for 2–5 days. Store them in the refrigerator for 3–6 months. To can, heat the fermented kimchi to simmering (185°F–210°F) and pack it into clean, hot jars, leaving ½ inch of headspace. Seal and process the jars for 15 minutes.

The gochugaru chili powder brings the spice and a bit of fruity smokiness to this Kimchi.

Green Tomato Chutney

Enhance the flavor of cheese sandwiches, grilled meats, or a cheese board with this green tomato chutney.

Makes: 3 pints • **Prep time:** 7 minutes • **Cook time:** 70 minutes • **Processing time:** 5 minutes at 0–1,000 ft elevation

Ingredients

- 2½ pounds firm green tomatoes, about 6 cups diced
- 1 cup golden raisins (or if you can find them, ½ cup currants)
- 1 cup chopped onion
- 1½ cups light brown sugar, firmly packed
- 1 teaspoon salt
- 1¼ cups cider vinegar
- 1 Tablespoon mixed pickling spices
- 1 teaspoon chili powder
- 1 Tablespoon chopped crystallized ginger

1. Dice tomatoes into ¾-inch pieces (you should have about 6 cups). Combine all ingredients in a large pot and bring to a boil. Reduce the heat and cook for about 1 hour, until thickened.
2. Spoon chutney into jars leaving ¼ inch of headspace and seal with a lid. Refrigerate up to three weeks or process for 5 minutes in a boiling water bath.

Giardiniera

Italian giardiniera uses a combination of olive oil and vinegar, with the vegetables left bite-sized to be enjoyed as an appetizer. Chicago's trademark giardiniera is chopped vegetables packed in olive oil (and don't forget a pepper for heat!). No matter the origin, every giardiniera benefits from marinating a few days in the fridge before canning or consumption. I know, I know. It's going to be hard to wait that long.

Makes: 2 pints • **Prep time:** 5 mins. • **Inactive prep time:** 48 hrs. • **Processing time:** 10 mins.

Ingredients

- 1 tablespoon salt, plus ½ cup
- 1 cup cauliflower (about ¼ head), chopped
- 2 celery stalks, chopped
- 2 carrots, chopped
- 1 bell pepper, seeded and chopped
- 1 jalapeño, seeded and chopped
- 1 cup white wine vinegar
- 2 tablespoons extra-virgin olive oil
- 3 cloves garlic, minced
- ¾ teaspoon dried oregano
- 3–4 green olives, chopped

1. Sprinkle 1 tablespoon of salt over the chopped vegetables and cover them with water. Let them soak overnight. Drain the brine and add the remaining ingredients to the cauliflower mixture.
2. Transfer the mixture to clean, sterilized jars. If using within 2 weeks, store the jars in the refrigerator. If canning, wipe the rims of the jars with a clean paper towel, leaving at least ½ inch of headspace, and seal them with lids. Process the jars in a boiling water bath for 10 minutes. Store in a dry, cool place for up to 6 months.

Tangy Hot Sauce

Fermenting hot sauce mellows the flavor of the peppers and gives the sauce a tangy finish. The carbohydrates in the peppers are converted into lactic acid, making the peppers easier to digest, and their nutrients more bioavailable. Increasing the fermentation time makes the mixture more sour and increases the acid content.

Makes: 1 quart • **Prep time:** 10 mins. • **Inactive prep time:** 24–120 hrs.

Ingredients

- 1 pound mixed peppers (poblano, jalapeño, serrano, habanero)
- 6 cloves garlic
- 2 tablespoons salt
- 1 tablespoon maple syrup
- ½ cup filtered water
- 1 cup white vinegar

1. Using gloves, cut the stems from the peppers and remove the seeds and pith. Add the peppers, garlic, salt, and maple syrup to a food processor or blender. Pulse until pureed, about 90 seconds.
2. Transfer the pepper mixture to a clean quart mason jar and top it with the water, leaving at least ½ inch of headspace. Cover the jar with a cheesecloth and secure it with a rubber band. Let it sit at room temperature for at least 24 hours, up to 2 weeks.
3. Check on the sauce every day, looking for tiny bubbles and taking a smell/taste test. Once the sauce has developed a flavor you enjoy, seal the jar with a lid and store it in the refrigerator for up to 2 months.

Pickled Jalapeños

Pickled jalapeños are a Texas staple. Texans add them to hamburgers, atop quesadillas and nachos, in sandwiches, and chopped up in salsa. Try adding minced pickled jalapeños to your egg salad to give it a vinegary kick.

Makes: 2 pints • **Prep time:** 10 mins. • **Cook time:** 10 mins. • **Processing time:** 10 mins.

Ingredients

- 2 cups white wine vinegar
- 2 cups filtered water
- ¼ cup honey
- 2 tablespoons salt
- 6 cloves garlic
- 1½ pounds (about 2 dozen) jalapeños

1 Place the vinegar, water, honey, salt, and garlic in a saucepan over high heat.
2 While the mixture heats, put on plastic gloves and slice the jalapeños into ¼-inch slices. Once the mixture comes to a boil, add in the jalapeños. Stir the mixture and remove the pan from heat.
3 Transfer the jalapeños to sanitized jars, leaving ½ inch of headspace, and seal with lids. Process the jars in a boiling water bath for 10 minutes, or store them in the refrigerator for up to 6 months.

Pickled Watermelon Rind

What's sweet, sour, and a great use for watermelon rinds? Popular in the South, pickled watermelon rind recipes date back to the mid-1800s. Jalapeño gives this some heat. Enjoy this preserve on top of sausage dogs, as an unexpected relish for cheese trays, or in sandwiches or salads.

Makes: 1½ quarts • **Prep time:** 20 mins. • **Cook time:** 15 mins. • **Processing time:** 10 mins.

Ingredients

- 2 pounds watermelon rinds, green skin removed, diced
- 2 tablespoons salt
- ½ cup apple cider vinegar
- ½ cup white vinegar
- 1 cup granulated sugar
- 3 cinnamon sticks
- 1-inch piece of ginger, peeled and grated
- 1 jalapeño, diced

1. Combine the watermelon rinds and salt in a non-reactive ceramic or plastic bowl. Store it in the refrigerator overnight, about 8 hours.

2. Remove the rinds from the refrigerator and transfer them to a strainer. Rinse the watermelon with running water. In a medium pot, combine the vinegars, sugar, and cinnamon sticks over high heat. Once boiling, add the watermelon, ginger, and jalapeño and cook for 10 minutes. Turn off the heat and let the pot sit for an additional 10 minutes, or until tender.

3. Transfer the mixture to sterilized jars, leaving ½ inch of headspace, and seal the jars. Refrigerate them for up to 2 weeks, or process for 10 minutes in a boiling water bath for long-term storage.

Classic Chowchow

Use the last of the season's cabbage and the first green tomatoes in this classic southern recipe, chowchow. Enjoy chowchow on top of a sausage dog, on a Rueben sandwich, or as part of a relish tray.

Makes: 3 pints • **Prep time:** 25 mins. • **Cook time:** 25 mins. • **Processing time:** 10 mins

Ingredients

- 2 teaspoons mustard seeds
- 2 teaspoons black peppercorns
- 1 teaspoon whole cloves
- 1½ cups granulated sugar
- 1 tablespoon pickling salt
- 1½ cups distilled white vinegar
- 1½ cups apple cider vinegar
- 1 teaspoon ground mustard
- 1 teaspoon ground turmeric
- ½ teaspoon ground cinnamon
- ½ teaspoon ground ginger
- ½ teaspoon red pepper flakes
- ½ head cabbage, shredded
- 3 cups green tomatoes, chopped
- 2 bell peppers, diced
- 1 sweet onion, diced

1. In a large pot, toast the mustard seeds, peppercorns, and cloves over medium heat for 5 minutes, shaking the pot occasionally, until the seeds are toasted and fragrant. Add the sugar, salt, vinegars, and spices to the pot and turn up the heat to high. Stirring frequently to dissolve the sugar and salt, cook for about 10 minutes, until the mixture comes to a boil.

2. Add the cabbage and chopped vegetables to the pot and bring it back to a boil. Reduce the heat to medium-low to simmer for an additional 10 minutes.

3. Transfer the chowchow into sterilized jars, leaving ½ inch of headspace. Seal and process the jars in a boiling water bath for 10 minutes.

Herbed Onion Marmalade

Vidalia or Texas 1015 onions work beautifully in this recipe. Try this marmalade on pork chops, homemade pizza, or with cream cheese on crackers.

Makes: 1 pint • **Prep time:** 10 mins. • **Cook time:** 45 mins. • **Processing time:** 10 mins.

Ingredients

- 4 tablespoons butter
- 4 medium yellow onions, thinly sliced
- 1 teaspoon salt
- ¼ teaspoon freshly ground black pepper
- ⅓ cup brown sugar
- ½ cup white wine vinegar
- ¼ teaspoon thyme
- 2 bay leaves
- 1 sprig rosemary

1. In a large pot, heat the butter, onion, salt, and pepper over low heat. Stirring occasionally, cook the onions until they become a light brown tawny color, about 30 minutes. Add the remaining ingredients and continue to cook until the liquid is reduced, about 15 minutes. Remove the bay leaves.
2. Transfer the marmalade to clean jars, leaving ¼ inch of headspace, and seal the jars with lids. Refrigerate for up to 4 days, or process in a boiling water bath for 5 minutes for long-term storage.

Essential Vegetable Broth

Cooking sustainably can be easy, as with this recipe for vegetable broth. Transform onion and garlic skins, carrot tops, and vegetable peels and stems into a rich broth with little effort and minimal expense. Store vegetable scraps in a freezer bag in the freezer until you have at least 2 cups' worth.

Makes: 5 pints • **Prep time:** 10 mins. • **Cook time:** 50 mins. • **Processing time:** 20 mins.

Ingredients

- 1 tablespoon olive oil
- 2 ribs celery, chopped
- 3 carrots, chopped
- 1 onion, chopped
- 5 cloves garlic, minced
- 2 teaspoons salt
- 2–3 cups reserved vegetable scraps

- 10 cups filtered water
- 1 ounce fresh parsley (or 1 tablespoon dried parsley)
- 5 sprigs fresh thyme (or 2 teaspoons dried thyme)

- 4 sprigs fresh rosemary (or 1½ teaspoons dried rosemary)
- 2 bay leaves
- 1 tablespoon Worcestershire sauce
- 1 tablespoon peppercorns

1. Heat a stockpot over medium-high heat. Add the olive oil and heat it for 2 minutes before adding the celery, carrots, and onion. Sauté for 4 minutes, stirring frequently, then add the garlic and salt. Cook for 1 minute to brown the garlic before adding the remaining ingredients.
2. Cover the pot with a lid and heat the broth to a boil, then reduce the heat to low and simmer, uncovered, for 45 minutes, to develop the flavors. Strain the broth into a pitcher using a fine-mesh colander.
3. Transfer the broth to the jars, leaving 1 inch of headspace, and seal the jars with lids. The broth will keep for 5 days in the refrigerator. Process the jars in a boiling water bath for 20 minutes for long-term storage.

Try adding chicken bones to create a rich meat-based broth from this delicious vegetable base.

Flavorful Stewed Tomatoes

Stewed tomatoes make a flavorful base for everything from chili to enchiladas. Add basil and oregano and puree to create an epic marinara sauce.

Makes: 2 quarts • **Prep time:** 15 mins. • **Cook time:** 20 mins. • **Processing time:** 35 mins.

Ingredients

- 5 pounds fresh tomatoes
- 2 tablespoons olive oil
- 2 tablespoons butter
- 1 large onion, chopped
- 1 bell pepper, chopped
- 1 fennel stalk, chopped
- 4 cloves garlic, minced
- 1½ teaspoons salt
- ½ teaspoon red pepper flakes
- 1 teaspoon citric acid (or 2 tablespoons bottled lemon juice)

1. Fill a large pot with water at least 4 inches deep over high heat. After removing their stems, rinse the tomatoes and cut a large X into each tomato skin. When the water starts to boil, cook each tomato for 1–2 minutes and remove it with a slotted spoon, then transfer it to a cold-water bath. Peel the tomatoes and cut them into quarters.

2. In a clean large pot, heat the olive oil and butter over medium heat. Once the butter has melted, add the onion, bell pepper, and fennel. Cook for 5 minutes, until the onion is fragrant and becoming translucent. Add the garlic and cook for 30 seconds. Add the tomatoes, salt, red pepper flakes, and citric acid and cook for 10 minutes, stirring frequently, until the tomatoes have broken down. Transfer the stewed tomatoes to clean, sterilized jars, leaving 1 inch of headspace.

3. Store the tomatoes in the refrigerator for up to 2 weeks. To can, transfer the tomatoes to clean, hot jars, leaving ½ inch of headspace. Seal then process the jars in a boiling water bath for 35 minutes.

Healthier Ketchup

My daughters love ketchup. They put it on pretty much every type of meat and potato I put in front of them. They've tried it on mac and cheese and scrambled eggs. I've caught my baby girl eating it by the spoonful. I decided, for my kids and my conscience, that I needed to make a ketchup that didn't have high-fructose corn syrup as its third ingredient. And this ketchup tastes so much better!

Makes: 1 quart • **Prep time:** 5 mins. • **Cook time:** 10 mins. • **Processing time:** 15 mins.

Ingredients

- 1 onion, chopped
- 3 garlic cloves, chopped
- 16 ounces stewed tomatoes
- 1 tablespoon olive oil
- 6 ounces tomato paste
- ¼ cup red wine vinegar
- 2 tablespoons brown sugar
- 2 tablespoons honey
- 1 tablespoon fish sauce
- 1 teaspoon dry mustard
- 1 teaspoon sea salt
- ½ teaspoon black or cayenne pepper

1. Combine the onion, garlic, and stewed tomatoes in a blender or food processor and puree for 1 minute.
2. Heat the olive oil in a medium saucepan over medium heat. Add the puree and bring it to a boil, stirring frequently. Boil for 1 minute, the add the remaining ingredients and bring to a boil.
3. Transfer the ketchup to sanitized jars, leaving ¼ inch of headspace, and seal the jars with lids. Refrigerate them for up to 2 weeks, or process them for 15 minutes for long-term storage.

Easy Strawberry Jam

Berries don't do well in our small, coastal town. The hot wind dries out the sandy soil before tender strawberry plants can set fruit. As soon as the struggling strawberries set fruit, the birds seize them. A good strawberry harvest at our house is a small handful of unripened, juiceless berries, each no bigger than a nickel. But strawberry jam is my daughter Emma's favorite, so we occasionally make the two-hour drive to Poteet, the "Strawberry Capital of Texas." A few bushels of Poteet strawberries make better jam than anything we can get at the grocery store.

Makes: 6 half-pints • **Prep time:** 10 mins. • **Cook time:** 20 mins. • **Processing time:** 10 mins.

Ingredients

- 3 pounds fresh strawberries
- 4 cups granulated sugar
- 3 tablespoons powdered fruit pectin*
- ¼ cup bottled lemon juice, plus two seeded lemon wedges
- Pinch of salt

To ensure the jam sets, use the following ratio of ingredients: 8 cups fruit, 6 cups sugar, 2 tablespoons pectin, and ¼ cup lemon juice.

1. Prepare the strawberries by rinsing them, removing their stems, and roughly chopping them. In a large pot, combine all of the ingredients over medium heat.
2. Stirring frequently and mashing the berries with the back of a spoon, bring the mixture to a boil and cook for 3 minutes, until the jam has thickened, approximately 20 minutes in total.
3. Remove the lemon wedges from the jam and skim off the foam from the top, if desired. Transfer the jam to clean, sterilized jars, leaving about ¼ inch of headspace at the top of each jar, and seal them with lids and rings.
4. Prepared jam can be stored in the refrigerator for up to 2 months, or at room temperature for 12 months if processed for 10 minutes in a boiling water bath. Discard any jars that have not sealed within 24 hours.

Blueberry Plum Jam

Hands down, this is my favorite jam. Maybe it's the balance of tart and sweet, or the hints of floral vanilla, but this is my jam (pun intended)!

Makes: 2 half-pints • **Prep time:** 15 mins. • **Cook time:** 20 mins. • **Processing time:** 10 mins.

Ingredients

- 1½ pounds plums, pitted and chopped into ½-inch pieces
- 18 ounces fresh or frozen blueberries
- 1 cup granulated sugar
- 1 vanilla bean
- Juice of 1 lemon

1. Combine all of the ingredients in a large pot over medium-high heat (215°F–220°F). Bring the mixture to a boil, stirring frequently to dissolve the sugar. Boil for 7–10 minutes. Test the mixture for doneness by dipping a cold spoon in the mixture and running your finger down the back of the spoon. Once your finger makes a distinct line through the liquid that doesn't blur back together, the preserves are done cooking. If the jam remains runny, simmer an additional 2–3 minutes.

2. Transfer the jam to clean, sterilized jars, leaving about ¼ inch of headspace at the top of each jar, and seal them with lids.

3. Prepared jam can be stored in the refrigerator for up to 2 months, or at room temperature for 12 months if processed for 10 minutes in a boiling water bath. Discard any jars that did not seal within 24 hours.

Spiced Applesauce

Is there anything better than sweet, spicy applesauce? It's a perfect healthy dessert, it works well if you're trying to add fruit to your breakfasts, and it makes a terrific mid-day snack.

Makes: 1 quart • **Prep time:** 10 mins. • **Cook time:** 15–20 mins. • **Processing time:** 15 mins.

Ingredients

- 8 apples, peeled, cored, and chopped
- ¼ cup maple syrup
- Pinch of salt
- Juice of 1 lemon
- ¼ teaspoon cinnamon

1. Add all of the ingredients to a large pot over medium heat. Stir to combine and cook, covered, for 15–20 minutes. Mash everything with a potato masher, or blend to the desired consistency in a food processor.
2. Transfer the applesauce to sterilized, hot jars, leaving ½ inch of headspace, and seal with lids. Process for 15 minutes.

Mostarda

Classic Italian *mostarda* is a mixture of fruit and mustard seeds that takes several steps and all day to prepare. This shortcut recipe is just as flavorful and takes only 30 minutes. Serve mostarda with charcuterie, braised meats, or on toasted bread.

Makes: 2 cups • **Prep time:** 7 mins. • **Cook time:** 30 mins. • **Processing time:** 10 mins.

Ingredients

- 1 tablespoon butter
- 1 shallot, minced
- 1 cup fresh fruit (mango, grapes, apples, peaches)
- ¼ cup dried fruit (apricots, golden raisins, cherries), chopped
- ½ cup dry white wine
- ¼ cup white wine vinegar
- ¼ cup water
- ¼ cup sugar
- ½ teaspoon salt
- 1 tablespoon Dijon mustard

1. Melt the butter over medium heat in a saucepan. Add the shallots and sweat them until they are tender and golden. Add in the remaining ingredients and simmer until the liquids have reduced and thickened, about 20 minutes. Mostarda is ready when the fruit is tender and the spread has the consistency of jam.
2. Pour the hot mostarda into sterilized, hot half-pint jars, leaving ½ inch of headspace. Seal and process the jars for 10 minutes in a boiling water bath.

Spring

Spring is a time for newness and rebirth. Plants and animals awaken to longer days and disappearing frost. While much of the northern hemisphere remains dormant with melting snow, March is an active month for us Southern gardeners.

We get our best showings of onions, peas, and spinach in early spring. Herbs flourish in spring's moderate temperatures and higher rainfall. As spring progresses and temperatures rise, we rely on fruit trees like avocado and banana to tide us over until the summer harvest begins to trickle in. Gardeners in moderate and cool climates might harvest the last of their apples for pies or applesauce to last them until next season.

I find myself more active in the kitchen (and in the garden) during these warmer months. Our pigs seem spryer and our chickens more vocal. Even our elderly farm cat, who has lazed on the windowsill for weeks, ventures outside for a pounce at that grasshopper she's been eyeing.

We're all familiar with joys of spring—sprouts rise up and flourish, fueling fresh, light meals to lift the spirit.

In Season

Artichokes	Collards	Mushrooms
Asparagus	Garlic	Onions
Avocados	Herbs	Peas
Bananas	Jicama	Radishes
Beets	Kale	Rhubarb
Broccoli	Leeks	Spinach
Cabbage	Lemons	Strawberries
Carrots	Lettuce	Swiss chard
Celery	Limes	Turnips

Grilled Artichokes with Roasted Garlic Dip

Prepping fresh artichokes is the most intimidating part of cooking fresh artichokes. It needn't be. Leave a longer stem when you harvest your artichoke to act as a handle as you snip sharp tips with your kitchen shears.

Servings: 4 • **Prep time:** 10 mins. • **Cook time:** 30 mins.

Ingredients

- 2 fresh artichokes
- ½ cup fresh herbs (I recommend rosemary, basil, oregano, and/ or parsley)
- 1 head garlic, halved width-wise
- ¼ cup olive oil, plus more for drizzling
- ½ teaspoon salt, plus more to taste
- Black pepper, to taste
- ¼ teaspoon red pepper flakes
- Juice of 2 lemons

1. Preheat the oven to 400°F and the grill to medium-high heat. Trim the tips of the leaves from each artichoke. Cut the artichokes in half lengthwise and remove the chokes. Brush the artichoke and garlic halves with olive oil and season them with salt and black pepper.
2. Place the garlic on a baking sheet and place it in the oven. Meanwhile, grill the artichokes for 7 minutes, cut sides down. Transfer the artichokes to the baking sheet in the oven and cook for 20 minutes, until the artichokes and the garlic are tender.
3. Blend the garlic with the herbs, olive oil, salt, red pepper flakes, and the juice of one lemon. Squeeze fresh lemon juice on top of the artichokes and serve with roasted garlic dipping sauce.

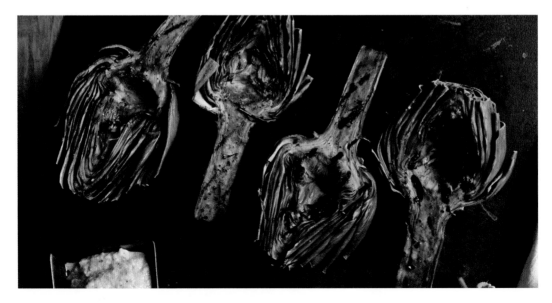

Asparagus Orzo

Every host should have a fail-proof dish that is a guaranteed crowd-pleaser. Asparagus orzo is mine. I like to toss in some shrimp or sautéed chicken for a one-pot meal.

Servings: 4 • **Prep time:** 3 mins. • **Cook time:** 15 mins.

Ingredients

- 8 ounces orzo
- 1 pound asparagus, chopped
- ¼ cup butter
- 3 cloves garlic, minced
- ½ cup Parmigiano Reggiano, plus more to serve
- Juice and zest of 1 lemon
- Salt and black pepper, to taste

1. Heat 3 cups of water over high heat. Season the water with 1 tablespoon of salt, or as preferred. Once the water is boiling, add the orzo and cook for 7 minutes. Add the asparagus and cook for 3 minutes. Strain the mixture and set it aside.
2. Return the pot to the stove and melt the butter over low heat. Add the garlic, Parmigiano Reggiano, lemon zest, salt and pepper and cook until the cheese is melted and the garlic is fragrant, about 1–2 minutes. Stir in the orzo and asparagus until they are nice and coated. Top with the extra cheese and lemon juice before serving.

Chard-Stuffed Manicotti

Dress up this manicotti with ground pork or substitute the chard for spinach or kale—in my opinion you can't mess up manicotti. But do make it easier on yourself and use a pastry or plastic bag fitted with a large pipette tip (or a dime-sized hole) to fill them.

Servings: 4–6 • **Prep time:** 7 mins. • **Cook time:** 40 mins.

Ingredients

- 8 ounces manicotti
- 1 tablespoon salt, plus 1 teaspoon
- 1 tablespoon olive oil
- 1 pound (about 4 cups) Swiss chard, stemmed and chopped
- 4 cups shredded mozzarella, divided
- ½ cup Parmigiano Reggiano, divided
- ¼ cup fresh parsley, finely chopped
- 2 tablespoons fresh mint, finely chopped
- 2 tablespoons fresh basil, finely chopped, plus more for garnish
- ½ teaspoon freshly ground black pepper
- 32 ounces whole-milk ricotta
- 16 ounces marinara sauce

1. Preheat the oven to 350°F. In a large pot, bring 5 quarts of water to a rapid boil over high heat and season it with salt. Add half of the pasta and stir the pot. Allow the water to reach a boil again before adding the second half of the pasta. Cook uncovered, stirring occasionally, for about 6 minutes. Strain the pasta in a colander and rinse with cold water. Lay the pasta in a single layer on wax paper to prevent it from sticking together.
2. In a large rimmed pan, heat the olive oil over medium heat. Add the chard and stir until it has wilted. Add 1–2 tablespoons of water as necessary to prevent the leaves from sticking to the pan. Remove the pan from heat and let it cool.
3. Combine 2 cups of the mozzarella, ¼ cup Parmigiano Reggiano, the herbs, 1 teaspoon of salt, and pepper into a large bowl, along with sautéed chard. Stir the mixture well and spoon it into a large piping bag or plastic bag with a corner cut off. Pipette the cheese mixture into the cooled manicotti and place them in a single layer in a 9 × 13-inch baking dish. Spoon marinara sauce evenly over the stuffed manicotti, and sprinkle on the remaining mozzarella and Parmigiano Reggiano. Bake for 25–30 minutes, until the cheese is melted and bubbly.

Leek and Mushroom Risotto

A simple recipe like this benefits from taking special care in choosing its ingredients. Earthy mushrooms like portobello, porcini, and shiitake stand up better to leeks than other varieties. Deglaze the pan with pinot grigio or a dry sauvignon blanc. Save the chardonnay for the next visit from the in-laws.

Servings: 8 • **Prep time:** 5 mins. • **Cook time:** 25 mins.

Ingredients

- 6 tablespoons olive oil
- 2 leeks, washed and chopped
- ¾ teaspoon salt
- 8 cups chicken broth
- 2 cups arborio rice
- ¾ pound mushrooms
- ½ cup dry white wine
- 2 cups Parmigiano Reggiano
- 2 teaspoons fresh thyme

1. Heat the olive oil in a large saucepan over medium heat for 2–3 minutes. Add the leeks and salt. Cook the leeks until they begin to turn translucent, 5–7 minutes, stirring frequently.
2. Meanwhile, heat the chicken broth in a separate stockpot over medium heat.
3. Add the rice and mushrooms to the leeks and cook for 2–3 minutes, until the rice becomes fragrant. Deglaze the plan with the white wine and cook until all the moisture has evaporated.
4. Ladle 1 cup of hot broth into the pan with the rice mixture. Stir the mixture frequently, until the stock has been absorbed. Continue to add stock in this fashion until the rice has started to become creamy but is still al dente in the very center, about 15 minutes.
5. Stir in the cheese and thyme until well incorporated. Serve the risotto warm, as an entree or side dish.

Garlic Herb Butter

It would be so easy to throw all the garlic and herbs into a food processor and press "pulse." Don't. The gnashing and grinding of a mortar and pestle can't be duplicated by steel blades. Plus, it just feels good to use your hands to create something wonderful.

Makes: 1 cup • **Prep time:** 7 mins.

Ingredients

- 8 cloves garlic, chopped
- 1 teaspoon salt
- ½ teaspoon cracked pepper
- 1 teaspoon lemon zest
- ½ cup unsalted butter, softened
- ¼ cup chopped chives, basil, and parsley

1. Using a mortar and pestle, grind together the garlic, salt, pepper, and lemon zest.
2. Stir the chopped herbs and the garlic mixture into the softened butter. Serve on crusty bread, roast potatoes and vegetables, or grilled meat. The butter can be stored up to 2 weeks in the refrigerator.

Bacon Leek Tart

Enjoy this tart cooled or at room temperature, on a Sunday with family or for dinner while watching your favorite show. There's magic in the mixture (it's probably the goat cheese).

Servings: 6–8 • **Prep time:** 20 mins. • **Inactive prep time:** 30–45 mins. • **Cook time:** 50 mins.

Ingredients

For the crust
- 1¼ cups all-purpose flour
- ½ teaspoon salt
- 1 teaspoon sugar
- ½ cup butter, cubed
- 4–6 tablespoons ice-cold water

For the filling
- ½ pound thick-cut bacon, chopped
- 2 tablespoons butter
- 2 leeks, peeled, rinsed, and chopped
- ½ cup heavy cream
- 3 large eggs
- 2 ounces goat cheese
- 1 tablespoon all-purpose flour
- 1 teaspoon thyme
- ¾ teaspoon salt
- ¼ teaspoon pepper
- ½ cup white cheddar, shredded

1. To make the crust, combine the flour, salt, and sugar in a food processor and pulse to mix. Add in the butter and pulse for 10 seconds, until the mixture has an oatmeal consistency. Add 4 tablespoons of water and pulse to combine. The dough is ready when it easily comes together without falling back apart. Add additional water, one tablespoon at a time, if necessary, until a smooth dough is formed. Form the dough into a disk, cover it with plastic wrap, and refrigerate it for 30–45 minutes.
2. Preheat the oven to 375°F. Remove the dough from the refrigerator and roll it out to a ¼-inch thickness on a floured surface. Transfer the crust to a fluted tart pan or pie pan and decorate the edges as desired. Prick the dough across its surface with a fork, or weigh the crust down with pie weights. Bake it for 20 minutes, until it is golden brown. Remove it from the oven and let it cool on a rack.
3. To make the filling, cook the bacon over medium heat until it is crisp. Transfer it to a paper towel–lined plate with a slotted spoon. Discard all but about 2 tablespoons of the bacon grease, then add the butter and leeks. Sauté the leeks until they are golden and transparent, about 5–7 minutes.
4. Combine the remaining ingredients in a blender or food processor and blend until combined. Stir in the reserved bacon and the leeks. Pour the mixture into the prepared crust and bake for 30 minutes, or until the filling is set.

Grass-Fed Steak with Summer Vegetables

This one-skillet wonder comes together with a flavor powerhouse—chimichurri. This verdant sauce is packed with fresh herbs and garlic—great for meat and vegetables alike.

Servings: 2 • **Prep time:** 3 mins. • **Cook time:** 20 mins.

Ingredients

- Chimichurri Sauce (see opposite page)
- 1–2-pound grass-fed beef steak (at least 1 inch in thickness), at room temperature
- Salt and freshly ground black pepper, to taste
- 2 corn cobs, husks removed, sliced horizontally
- 2 zucchini, sliced into spears
- 4 tablespoons butter
- 4 cloves garlic

1. Prepare the chimichurri sauce (see opposite page).
2. Preheat a seasoned cast-iron skillet on high heat. Season the steak liberally with salt and pepper, then cook the steak for 4 minutes on each side for medium-rare.
3. Sprinkle salt and pepper over the vegetables and add them to the pan while the steak is cooking, turning them frequently to prevent burning.
4. Remove the steak and allow it to rest for about 10 minutes. Continue to cook the vegetables until they are tender and lightly charred on all sides. Set the vegetables aside and reduce the heat to low.
5. Add the butter and garlic to the skillet, scraping the bottom of the pan to release any flavorful bits.
6. To serve, drizzle the steak with garlic butter and a spoonful of chimichurri sauce.

Chimichurri Sauce

Ingredients

- 1 bunch fresh parsley (about 2 ounces)
- ⅓ cup red wine vinegar
- 4 garlic cloves
- ¾ teaspoon salt
- ½ teaspoon red pepper flakes
- ½ cup extra-virgin olive oil

1. In a blender or food processor, pulse the parsley, vinegar, garlic, salt, and red pepper flakes until smooth.
2. With the blender still on, add the olive oil in a slow, steady stream until well incorporated. Let the flavors develop for 20 minutes before serving. Chimichurri will keep in an airtight container for 1 week.

Thai Coconut Seafood Soup

This soup pairs healthy fresh seafood with flavorful Thai ingredients to create a memorable dish. I made this soup for my husband early on in our courtship. He still mentions it in casual conversation 10 years later.

Servings: 6 • **Prep time:** 5 mins. • **Cook time:** 15 mins.

Ingredients

- 2 tablespoons coconut oil
- 6 cloves garlic
- 1 tablespoon ginger
- 1 stalk lemongrass
- 4–8 Thai chiles
- 4 cups fish stock or chicken stock
- 2 (13.5 oz) cans coconut milk
- 3 tablespoons fish sauce
- 1 teaspoon salt
- Juice of 2 limes
- 1 tablespoon brown sugar
- 1 pound local fish filet, such as flounder
- ½ pound shrimp, peeled and deveined
- ½ pound mussels, debearded and cleaned
- ½ pound clams, cleaned
- 1 bunch fresh basil or cilantro

1. In a large pot, cook the coconut oil over medium heat. Sauté the garlic, ginger, lemongrass, and Thai chiles for 2 minutes. (For a milder soup, decrease the number of chiles or add them later in the cooking process).
2. Add the fish stock, coconut milk, fish sauce, salt, lime juice, and brown sugar to the pot and bring to a boil. Once boiling, add the fish, shrimp, mussels, and clams and cook for 3 minutes, until most of the shells have opened.
3. Remove from heat and serve with chopped basil or cilantro leaves.

Lemon Thyme Cake

I love the look of lemon zest sprinkled on the top of this cake, but admittedly the flavor may be too lemony for some. Tarragon is a suitable substitution

Serving: 1 large Bundt cake or six 4- to 5-inch Bundt cakes • **Prep time:** 10–15 mins. • **Cook time:** 25–30 mins.

Ingredients
For the cake batter
- 1 stick unsalted butter
- ¼ cup olive oil
- 1 cup sugar
- 2 eggs
- ½ cup all-purpose flour
- 1½ teaspoons baking powder
- 1 tablespoon lemon zest
- ¾ teaspoon salt
- ½ cup buttermilk
- 2 teaspoons vanilla extract
- 2 tablespoons lemon juice
- 2 tablespoons fresh thyme, plus more for garnish

For the lemon drizzle
- 1 cup powdered sugar
- Juice of 2 lemons (or ½ cup)

1. Preheat the oven to 350°F. Oil the Bundt cake pan(s) with nonstick baking spray.
2. Beat the butter, olive oil, and sugar with the paddle attachment of your stand mixer, or with a handheld electric mixer, until a yellow, fluffy, homogeneous mixture forms. Add the eggs one at a time, mixing until the first is fully incorporated before adding the second.
3. In a large bowl, whisk the flour, baking powder, lemon zest, and salt together until well combined. Add half of this dry mixture to the butter mixture. Add in ¼ cup of the buttermilk and mix well. Mix in the rest of the dry mixture, followed by the rest of the buttermilk. Finally, add the vanilla extract, lemon juice, and thyme to the batter and mix until well combined.
4. Pour the batter into the oiled Bundt cake pan. Bake for 25–30 minutes, or until the cake is golden brown and a toothpick inserted into the center comes out clean. Let the cake cool to room temperature.
5. To make the lemon drizzle, whisk the powdered sugar and lemon juice together until all lumps are gone. Drizzle generously on top of the cooled cake. Garnish with leaves of fresh thyme.

Balsamic Beet Salad with Feta and Pecans

Some helpful advice: try the candied pecans and balsamic vinaigrette on everything!

Servings: 2 • **Prep time:** 20 mins. • **Cook time:** 45 mins.

Ingredients
For the salad and candied pecans

- 1 pound beets, ends removed, cut into wedges
- Olive oil, as needed
- Salt and pepper, to taste
- ½ cup pecans
- ½ teaspoon cinnamon
- ½ teaspoon salt
- ¼ teaspoon cayenne
- 2 tablespoons maple syrup
- 3 cups tender greens (spinach, arugula, chard, beet greens)
- ½ red onion, thinly sliced
- 1 ounce crumbled feta
- 3 sprigs fresh dill

For the balsamic vinaigrette

- ¼ cup olive oil
- 2 tablespoons balsamic vinegar
- 1 tablespoon shallot, grated
- 1 clove garlic, grated
- 2 teaspoons honey
- 1 teaspoon Dijon mustard
- ¼ teaspoon salt
- ¼ teaspoon freshly ground black pepper

1. Preheat the oven to 375°F. Place the beet wedges on a baking sheet lined with parchment paper. Drizzle the olive oil over the beets and season them with salt and pepper. Roast them for 45 minutes, turning the wedges over halfway through. Let them cool for 10 minutes, or until they are cool to the touch.

2. Heat a pan over medium-low heat. Add the pecans in a single layer and cook for 3 minutes, stirring frequently. In a small bowl, mix together the cinnamon, salt, and cayenne. Add the spice mixture and syrup to the pecans and remove them from heat.

3. To make the vinaigrette, whisk all the ingredients together in a medium-size bowl. To assemble the salad, layer the greens and roasted beets, and top the salad with the candied pecans, onion, feta, and fresh dill. Drizzle with the vinaigrette and enjoy.

Kale Slaw

Crisp kale is the perfect base for a spring slaw. A quick aioli keeps this slaw from being too soggy or too sweet.

Servings: 6 • **Prep time:** 15 mins. • **Cook time:** 10 mins.

Ingredients

- ¾ cup sunflower seeds
- 1 egg yolk
- ¼ cup olive oil
- Juice of 1 lemon (about 2 tablespoons)
- 1 teaspoon Dijon mustard
- ½ teaspoon salt
- ¼ teaspoon freshly ground black pepper
- 1 teaspoon poppy seeds
- 1 tablespoon honey
- 1 cup kale, shredded
- 1 cup carrots, shredded
- 1 cup cabbage, shredded
- ¾ cup golden raisins

1. Preheat the oven to 400°F. Spread the sunflower seeds on a baking sheet and roast them for 5 minutes. Remove them from the oven and set aside.
2. In a medium bowl, beat the egg yolk well. Slowly drizzle olive oil into the egg yolk and whisk until well combined. Continue to add olive oil a little at a time while whisking, until the mixture reaches a mayonnaise consistency. Add the lemon juice, mustard, salt, pepper, poppy seeds, and honey and combine.
3. In a large bowl, combine the kale, carrots, and cabbage, fold in the poppy seed dressing, the golden raisins, and sunflower seeds. Serve with grilled oysters, fish, or barbecue.

This light, refreshing kale slaw is the perfect accompaniment to a fresh oyster bar!

Vegan Buddha Bowl

This recipe comes with a challenge: experiment until you find your favorite buddha bowl combination, then experiment some more.

Servings: 1 • **Prep time:** 30 mins. • **Cook time:** 30 mins.

Ingredients

- ½–1 cup dry legumes (lentils, beans, peas, or edamame)
- ½–¾ cup whole grains (couscous, brown rice, bulgur, millet, or amaranth)
- 1 cup fresh greens (spinach, kale, lettuce, chard, or arugula)
- 1–2 ounces healthy fat (avocado, nut butter, nuts, or olives)
- ½ cup cooked starchy vegetable (sweet potato, winter squash, pumpkin, or corn)
- 1 cup non-starchy vegetables (carrot, cucumber, celery, cauliflower, cabbage, radish, zucchini, pepper, tomato, beet, or jicama)
- Salt and pepper, to taste
- Citrus Basil Vinaigrette (optional, see recipe below)

1. Cook the dry legumes and whole grains according to package directions. Place the greens in a bowl.
2. Top with the remaining ingredients and season with salt and pepper. If desired, dress with your favorite dressing, oil and vinegar, or the citrus basil vinaigrette (see recipe).

Citrus Basil Vinaigrette

Ingredients

- 3 tablespoons olive oil
- 1 tablespoon freshly squeezed orange juice
- 1 tablespoon minced basil
- Salt and pepper, to taste

1. Whisk the ingredients together in a small bowl. Serve immediately, as dressing will naturally separate if stored or left out.

Vegan Spring Rolls

Versatile and refreshing, these spring rolls are great fresh or fried, vegan or with ground pork added. If you're new to the game and your rolls aren't picture-perfect, take heart. Practice makes perfect (and leaves you with a lot of leftovers to enjoy).

Servings: 8 rolls • **Prep time:** 40 mins.

Ingredients
For the spring rolls
- 1 (7–12 ounce) package rice paper wrappers
- 1 cup fresh spinach
- ½ cup red cabbage, julienned
- ½ cup carrots, julienned
- ⅓ cup jicama, thinly sliced
- ¼ cup Thai basil, julienned
- 1 medium avocado, thinly sliced
- 1 red bell pepper, seeded and thinly sliced

For the dipping sauce
- ½ cup soy sauce
- 1 teaspoon rice wine vinegar
- 1 tablespoon mirin
- 1 teaspoon brown sugar
- ½ teaspoon red chili paste

1. Fill a shallow bowl with water. Organize a large work space with sliced vegetables.
2. To make the spring rolls, immerse a rice paper wrapper in the water and let it soak for 15–20 seconds, until it is malleable. Spread the wrapper flat on your work surface. Starting on the side closest to you, add a small pile of each of the vegetables and herbs about ½ to 1 inch from the bottom of the wrapper.
3. Fold the edge of the wrapper over the vegetables, fold the sides in as if you were making an envelope, and continue to roll until the wrapper has formed a cylinder. Repeat until you have no ingredients remaining.
4. To make the dipping sauce, in a small bowl, combine the ingredients and mix until a cohesive sauce is formed. Spring rolls are best enjoyed fresh, with a side of dipping sauce.

Thai Lettuce Wraps

Harvest your lettuce when it's about the size of a dollar bill and still very crisp for optimal results.

Servings: 4 • **Prep time:** 15 mins. • **Cook time:** 10 mins.

Ingredients
For the pork filling
- 2 tablespoons sesame seed oil
- ½ onion, chopped
- 1 jalapeño, mostly seeded, finely minced
- 1 pound ground pork
- Pinch of salt
- Red pepper flakes, to taste
- 2 garlic cloves, minced
- 1 heaping tablespoon fresh ginger, grated
- 6 tablespoons low-sodium soy sauce
- Generous splash of mirin
- Splash of rice wine vinegar
- 1 tablespoon packed brown sugar

For the wraps and toppings
- 12 large lettuce leaves, rinsed well and dried (I recommend Bibb leaves)
- 5 baby carrots, julienned
- Cabbage, shredded
- 1 bunch fresh cilantro
- Juice of 1 lime

1. Heat the oil in a sauté pan on medium heat.
2. Add the onion and jalapeño, sautéing until tender. Add the pork, salt, and red pepper flakes. When the pork is almost completely browned, add the garlic and ginger, cooking for 1 minute, until fragrant. Stir in the liquids and brown sugar. Increase the heat to high and cook until the liquids reach a rolling boil.
3. Remove the pan from heat. Finish with squeezed lime.
4. To assemble wraps, place a portion of the pork filling, carrot, and cabbage on a large lettuce leaf. Top with cilantro and finish with freshly squeezed lime juice. Repeat until no ingredients remain.

Peas with Herbs

This recipe is my answer to pea salad. It not that I don't love the mayo-based version, dotted with ham and cheddar cheese cubes, because it's always been a favorite. I wanted to create a dish where peas take center stage, though. Let me tell you, these freshly picked peas own the spotlight.

Servings: 4 • **Prep time:** 7 mins. • **Cook time:** 2 mins.

Ingredients

- 2 pounds fresh peas
- 1 teaspoon salt, plus more as needed
- ½ cup arugula
- ¼ cup parsley
- ¼ cup basil
- ¼ cup mint
- 2 tablespoons extra-virgin olive oil
- 2 cloves garlic
- ½ teaspoon black pepper
- Zest and juice of one lemon

1. Prepare an ice-water bath. In a medium saucepan, add the peas to boiling, salted water and cook for 1–2 minutes, until the peas are crisp-tender. Strain the peas and transfer them to the ice-water bath.
2. In your blender or food processor, combine the remaining ingredients and pulse for 30 seconds, until they are finely minced. Toss the peas with the pesto and squeeze lemon juice on top prior to serving.

Grilled Broccoli with Furikake

Who knew a recipe this simple could be so delicious? Furikake is a mixture of dried fish, seaweed, sesame seeds, and spices popular in Japan. It adds a wonderful umami saltiness that perfectly complements the charred broccoli. Try it!

Servings: 4 • **Prep time:** 5 mins. • **Cook time:** 20 mins.

Ingredients

- 1 head of broccoli
- 1 tablespoon sesame seed oil
- ½ teaspoons sea salt
- ¼ teaspoon freshly ground black pepper
- 1 tablespoon furikake

1. Preheat the grill per the manufacturer's instructions.
2. Slice the broccoli lengthwise, into about five ½-inch "steaks." Brush each slice with sesame oil and season with salt and pepper.
3. Grill the broccoli on medium, indirect heat for 8–10 minutes, until well-defined char marks appear.
4. Flip the broccoli over and cook for 8–10 minutes. Remove them from heat. Season the broccoli with furikake and serve as a side or entree.

Five Variations on Quiche

Quiche is endlessly versatile. This recipe makes a fantastic base for highlighting your freshest garden ingredients.

Makes: 1 quiche

Ingredients

- 1 store-bought pie crust
- 6 eggs (increase to 9 eggs if using a deep-dish pie pan)
- ¾ cup heavy cream (increase to 1 cup if using deep-dish pie pan)
- ½ teaspoon salt (increase to ¾ teaspoon if using deep-dish pie pan)
- ¼ teaspoon freshly ground black pepper
- 1½ cups shredded cheese (varies by recipe)
- 2 cups mix-ins (differs for each variation, see recipes)

1. Preheat the oven to 350°F. If you're using prepared crust dough, roll it out into a 12-inch circle. Transfer the dough to a 9-inch pie plate and fold over the edges, crimping with your fingers or the tines of a fork.
2. In a large bowl, whisk together the whole eggs, heavy cream, salt, and pepper. Stir in 1 cup of shredded cheese and the mix-ins.
3. Pour the egg mixture into the prepared pie crust. Top with the remaining ½ cup of cheese.
4. Bake for 40–50 minutes (60 minutes for a deep-dish pie pan), until the center of the quiche is set.

Bacon and Brussels Sprouts Quiche
Mix-Ins

- ½ pound bacon, cut into 1-inch pieces
- 1 cup Brussels sprouts, thinly sliced
- ½ cup goat cheese
- 1 cup mozzarella

1. In a large pan, sauté the bacon for 2–3 minutes.
2. Add in the Brussels sprouts and cook for 10 minutes, until the bacon is crisp and the sprouts have begun to turn golden.
3. Stir most of the bacon, the Brussels sprouts, goat cheese, and ½ cup mozzarella into the egg custard and pour it into the prepared pie crust. Top with an additional ½ cup mozzarella and extra bacon bits.

Garlicky Kale Quiche
Mix-Ins

- 2 tablespoons olive oil
- 4 cloves garlic, minced
- 1 bunch kale, stemmed and chopped
- 4 ounces shredded Parmesan
- 4 ounces ricotta

1. Heat the oil in a large sauté pan. Once the oil is hot and shimmering, add the garlic and kale. Cook for 2–3 minutes, stirring frequently, until the garlic is fragrant and the kale has wilted.
2. Add the mixture to the egg custard, along with the cheeses, and proceed with the master recipe.

Summer's Harvest Quiche

Mix-Ins

- 1 pound eggplant
- 1 large tomato
- 1 bell pepper
- ½ onion
- 1 teaspoon salt
- 2 tablespoons olive oil
- 1 teaspoon Italian herbs
- 1 ½ cups gruyere

1. Slice the eggplant, tomato, bell pepper, and onion into ½-inch medallions. Lay the sliced eggplant and tomato on a paper towel–lined surface and sprinkle them with salt. Let them sit for 10 mins, then use another paper towel to pat the surface of the eggplant and tomato to remove any excess liquid.
2. Distribute the eggplant, bell pepper, and onion slices evenly over a rimmed baking sheet. Drizzle the vegetables with olive oil and sprinkle on herbs before baking in the oven for 15 minutes at 350°F, flipping the vegetables halfway through.
3. Proceed with the master recipe instructions for the egg filling, using 1 cup of gruyere cheese. Stir in the cooked vegetables and transfer the egg-vegetable mixture to the prepared pie crust. Top with the reserved tomato slices and ½ cup grated gruyere. Bake as instructed.

Asparagus and Prosciutto Quiche

Mix-Ins

- 5 ounces asparagus
- 1 cup gruyere
- ½ cup Parmesan
- 3 ounces prosciutto, torn into bite-size pieces

1. Cut the asparagus spears into 3 segments. Stir ½ cup of gruyere and the Parmesan cheese into the egg mixture.
2. Add in the asparagus and prosciutto. Top with the remaining gruyere prior to baking as instructed in the master recipe.

Zucchini and Ham Quiche

Mix-Ins

- 2 tablespoons butter
- 1 shallot, diced
- 1 zucchini, grated
- Salt and pepper, to taste
- 4 ounces cubed, cured ham
- 1 ½ cups shredded cheddar

1. Heat the butter in a large sauté pan over medium heat. Add the shallot and zucchini, stirring frequently until the vegetables are tender, about 5 minutes.
2. Season the mixture with salt and pepper before adding it to the egg custard, along with the ham and 1 cup cheddar cheese. For extra cheesy goodness, top the quiche with an additional ½ cup cheddar prior to baking as instructed.

Five Variations on Quiche • 79

Summer

For many, summer is the most productive time in the garden. The gallons of zucchini and ruby-red tomatoes make the time and preparation you've invested in your garden worth it.

Most of my garden is filled with the Native American "Three Sisters"—corn, beans, and squash. Blue Lake and Kentucky Wonder pole beans vine up heirloom dent corn, like Oaxacan Green and Cherokee White Eagle. Broad leaves of butternut, cushaw, and delicata squash create a canopy to trap in moisture and protect the crops from the oppressive heat. Cucumbers fastened with zip ties vine up large cattle fence panels. All await their time in the kitchen.

Peppers beg to be pickled, cucumbers are quickly chopped into an easy Greek salad, and a glut of squash goes best pan-seared in butter. Herbs brighten everything and it becomes a game to make the next dish more colorful than the last. The possibilities in the garden and the kitchen seem endless, until the heat becomes too much, and it is all you can do to put together a simple salad and take a rest with a tall glass of ice tea.

My husband refers to August and the beginning of September as "the winter of summer." It's an apt description for the six weeks when we can grow little more than black-eyed peas and okra. The soil is so hot, steam can billow up in mirages mid-afternoon. But how satisfying is it to sit in a circle of loved ones, shelling peas and planning the fall planting?

Summer will probably feel like your most productive time in the garden—colorful vegetables grow before your eyes, begging to be turned into delicious shareable dishes.

In Season

Apricots

Avocados

Bananas

Basil

Beets

Bell peppers

Blackberries

Blueberries

Cantaloupe

Carrots

Celery

Cherries

Corn

Cucumbers

Eggplant

Garlic

Green beans

Honeydew melon

Lemons

Lemon squash

Lima beans

Limes

Mangos

Okra

Peaches

Plums

Raspberries

Scallop squash

Strawberries

Striped zucchini

Tomatillos

Tomatoes

Watermelon

Yellow crookneck squash

Yellow straightneck squash

Yellow zucchini

Zucchini

Vegetable Calzone

Another adaptable recipe, fill these calzones with your favorite summer produce, mushrooms, arugula, shredded chicken, ground pork, pepperoni, sun-dried tomatoes, pesto, or anything that pleases you.

Makes: 4 calzones • **Prep time:** 20 mins. • **Cook time:** 20 mins.

Ingredients

For the dough
- 2 cups all-purpose flour
- 2½ teaspoons (1 packet) active dry yeast
- 1½ teaspoons sugar
- ¾ teaspoon salt
- ¼ teaspoon garlic powder
- ¼ teaspoon dried oregano
- ¾ cup warm water
- 2 tablespoons olive oil

For the filling
- 1 red onion, sliced
- 8 cloves garlic
- 3 cups spinach
- 2 bell peppers, sliced
- 1 zucchini, sliced
- 1 yellow squash, sliced
- 2 cups mozzarella
- 1 cup fresh basil
- Salt and pepper, to taste
- Serve with warm marinara sauce

1. Preheat the oven to 450°F. Grease a baking sheet with olive oil or line it with parchment paper.
2. In a large bowl, combine the dough ingredients and mix for 5 minutes to develop the gluten. Divide the dough into 4 balls and roll each into a circle 9 inches in diameter.
3. To make the filling, divide the ingredients evenly between the 4 dough circles. Add a quarter of the ingredients to half of one of the prepared crusts. Fold the dough over the filling and crimp the edges together with your fingers or by pressing with a fork. Repeat for the remaining calzones.
4. Transfer the calzones to the baking sheet and cut 2–3 small holes in the top of each to vent. Brush the tops with olive oil and bake for 15–20 minutes, until the crust is golden brown. Serve the calzones with warm marinara.

Shakshuka

Shakshuka is a North African dish where eggs are poached in tomato sauce. The addition of feta adds a salty creaminess to combat the peppery sauce. Omit or add more jalapeños or other regional chiles according to your preference.

Servings: 4–6 • **Prep time:** 5 mins. • **Cook time:** 30 mins.

Ingredients

- 2 tablespoons olive oil
- 1 medium onion, diced
- 1 red bell pepper, diced
- 1–2 jalapeños, seeded and minced
- 3 cloves garlic, minced
- 1 teaspoon cumin
- 1 tablespoon sweet paprika
- ½ teaspoon salt
- ¼ teaspoon cayenne
- 1 can whole tomatoes
- 8 eggs
- 4 ounces crumbled feta cheese
- ⅓ cup parsley or cilantro
- Serve with Pita Bread (see recipe on page 126) or crusty bread, warmed

1. In a large skillet, heat the olive oil over medium heat for 3 minutes. Add the onion and peppers, sautéing for 10 minutes. Add the garlic and spices and cook for 1 minute, stirring continually.
2. Stir in the tomatoes, breaking them apart with a wooden spoon. Bring the mixture to a simmer, then crack the eggs on top. Sprinkle feta cheese over the shakshuka.
3. Cover the pan and simmer for 10 minutes, or bake in the oven (preheated to 375°F) until the egg whites are opaque (about 10 minutes). Garnish with the fresh herbs and serve with warm pitas or your favorite crusty bread.

Vegan Bulgogi

Korean bulgogi, "fire meat," usually refers to grilled beef that has been thinly sliced and marinated in a sweet-and-savory sauce. If you do occasionally enjoy meat, sliced beef or pork tenderloin also makes a lovely addition to this vegan version for a satisfying one-pot meal.

Servings: 4 • **Prep time:** 10 mins. • **Cook time:** 10 mins.

Ingredients

- 3 tablespoons vegetable oil
- 1 pear, cored
- 1 Japanese eggplant, chopped
- 1 summer squash, chopped
- 1 zucchini, chopped
- 2 bell peppers, chopped
- 1 onion, chopped
- ⅓ cup soy sauce
- 3 tablespoons honey
- 2 tablespoons mirin
- 1 tablespoon sesame seed oil
- 1 tablespoon garlic
- 1 tablespoon ginger
- ½ teaspoons gochugaru flakes or 1 teaspoon gochujang
- Serve with green onions, sesame seeds, and steamed rice

1. Heat the oil over medium heat in a large sauté pan or wok. Add in the pear and all the vegetables and cook for 7 minutes, until they are fork tender.
2. While vegetables cook, add remaining ingredients to your food processor and blend until smooth. Add the sauce to sautéed vegetables and cook for 1–2 minutes, until the sauce thickens slightly.
3. Top the bulgogi with green onions and sesame seeds and serve over steamed rice.

Zucchini Fritters

Hide larger or tough-skinned zucchini in these crisp fritters. Serve warm as an appetizer or side.

Makes: 6 fritters • **Prep time:** 10 mins. • **Cook time:** 20 mins.

Ingredients

- 1 pound zucchini, ends removed
- 2 ears corn, husks removed
- 2 cloves garlic
- 1 cup panko bread crumbs
- 1 cup Parmigiano Reggiano, grated
- 1 teaspoon salt
- ½ teaspoon cayenne
- ½ teaspoon baking powder
- 3 eggs
- ¼ cup butter
- ½ cup cooking oil
- Serve with chopped green onions

1. Grate the zucchini into a fine mesh strainer lined with paper towels. Squeeze the zucchini through the paper towels to remove any excess liquid. Remove the paper towels and transfer the zucchini to a large bowl.
2. Place the corn end side down and cut the kernels off using a knife. Add the corn, bread crumbs, Parmigiano Reggiano, salt, cayenne, baking powder, and eggs to the large bowl containing the zucchini. Mix the ingredients until well combined.
3. Heat a deep-sided pan over medium heat. Add the butter and oil to pan. Once the butter is melted and hot (about 5 minutes), add ¼–⅓ cup of batter using a measuring cup and cook for 3–4 minutes on each side. Transfer the fried fritter to a paper towel–lined plate and repeat until all of the batter has been used. Serve immediately with chopped green onions.

Grilled Summer Vegetables with Feta and Oregano

Grilling vegetables caramelizes their natural sugars and imparts an *umami* smokiness while keeping them crisp and tender. I recommend Italian oregano for this dish, which is a more tender, sweeter variety, though chopped Greek, Turkish, or Mexican oregano varieties will also elevate this dish with an earthy vibrancy.

Servings: 4 • **Prep time:** 10 mins. • **Cooking time:** 20 mins.

Ingredients

- ½ red onion, cut into ½-inch slices
- 1 yellow straight-neck squash, sliced lengthwise into ½-inch thick slices
- 1 calabaza, sliced lengthwise into ½-inch thick slices
- 1 zucchini, sliced lengthwise into ½-inch thick slices
- ½ eggplant, cut into ½-inch slices
- ¼ cup olive oil
- ½ teaspoon salt
- ¼ teaspoon black pepper
- 2 ounces feta
- 1 bunch fresh oregano, torn

1. Preheat the grill to 400°F, or heat a cast-iron grill pan over medium-high heat.
2. Brush the vegetables with olive oil and season them with salt and pepper. Working in batches, grill the vegetables for 3 minutes on each side, until a nice sear forms and the vegetable is fork tender.
3. Arrange the cooked vegetables on a platter and drizzle them with olive oil. Top with the feta crumbles and oregano leaves and serve.

Squash and Eggplant Confit

Many vegetables can be prepared *confit*, the French method of cooking something slowly in butter or duck fat. Try this preparation with pumpkin or winter squash, as well.

Servings: 6 • **Prep time:** 5 mins. • **Cook time:** 60–75 mins.

Ingredients

- 1 pound summer squash, cut lengthwise into ⅓-inch slices
- 1 pound eggplant, cut lengthwise into ⅓-inch inch slices
- 1 teaspoon salt
- 8 cloves garlic, mashed, peeled, and roughly chopped
- 2 teaspoons thyme
- ½ cup salted butter, diced
- 1 cup olive oil
- Garnish: juice of 1 lemon

1. Preheat the oven to 300°F. Lay the slices of squash and eggplant on a tea towel lined with paper towels and season them with salt. Let the vegetables sit for 30 minutes. Blot any accumulated moisture from the vegetables with clean paper towels.
2. Arrange the slices on a rimmed baking sheet. Distribute the garlic, thyme, and butter evenly on top of the vegetables. Pour the olive oil evenly over vegetables.
3. Bake for 60–70 minutes until the vegetables are tender and start to become translucent. Garnish with a generous splash of freshly squeezed lemon juice.

Watermelon Granita

This granita is a lovely dish originally from Sicily. This frozen fruit dessert could be the love child of sorbet and shaved ice. Granita requires no special equipment or ingredients, only a little patience while the fruit slurry freezes.

Servings: 12 • **Prep time:** 15 mins. • **Inactive prep time:** 1 hr. 40 mins. •**Cook time:** 2 mins.

Ingredients
- ¾ cup water
- ½ cup sugar
- 7 cups watermelon, peeled and cubed
- 4 tablespoons lime juice (or juice of 2 limes)
- Small bunch fresh sweet basil (about 6 large leaves)

1. Place a 9 x 13-inch glass or metal dish in the freezer.
2. Place the water and sugar in a small saucepan over medium-high heat. Simmer while stirring with a whisk until all of the sugar is dissolved and the liquid reaches a syrup consistency, about 2 minutes. Let it cool to room temperature.
3. Combine the watermelon, simple syrup, lime, and basil in a food processor and pulse until smooth. Pour the mixture into the cooled pan and place it back in the freezer. Using a whisk, stir mixture every 20 minutes, until the desired consistency is reached, before serving.

Easiest Cucumber Salad

A friend invited my family to an impromptu barbecue with only a few hours' notice. As with this clean and uncomplicated salad, oftentimes the best innovation comes out of desperation.

Servings: 4 • **Prep time:** 15 mins. • **Inactive prep time:** 10 mins. • **Heat time:** 5 mins.

Ingredients

- ½ cup white wine vinegar
- ½ cup water
- 1 tablespoon sugar
- 1 teaspoon salt
- 2 cucumbers, sliced
- 1 red onion, thinly sliced
- Garnish: 1 bunch of mint, chopped

1. Combine the vinegar, water, sugar, and salt in a medium pot over high heat. Whisk the mixture until the sugar and salt have dissolved.
2. Remove the pot from heat, and let this mixture cool for 10 minutes.
3. Pour the mixture over the sliced cucumbers and onion and garnish with the mint.

Shrimp Salad

Loosely based on Mexican shrimp cocktail (*Coctel de Camarones*), this shrimp salad is a refreshing change of pace that requires minimal time in the kitchen. Increase the number of jalapeños or leave the seeds in for more heat, or leave them out altogether if you prefer. For a perfect summer cocktail hour, enjoy shrimp salad as an appetizer to fish tacos served with a margarita on the rocks.

- **Servings:** 4
- **Prep time:** 7 mins.
- **Cook time:** 3 mins.
- **Inactive prep time:** 15 mins.

Ingredients

- 2 pounds shrimp
- 1 pound assorted tomatoes, chopped
- 2 avocadoes, peeled, pitted, and diced
- 1 red onion, diced
- 2 jalapeños, seeded and minced
- ¼ cup lime juice
- ¾ teaspoon salt
- ¼ cup fresh basil, chopped

1. Bring salted water to boil in a large pot. Add the shrimp and boil for 2–3 minutes, until the shrimp are no longer opaque.
2. Strain the shrimp, transfer it to a large bowl, and refrigerate it for 10–15 minutes. Combine the cooled shrimp with the remaining ingredients and serve chilled.

Grilled Fish Tacos with Cucumber Slaw and Basil Pico de Gallo

The fresh flavors, colors, and textures of these fish tacos have become my favorite compilation album of summer. My family and I eat them on repeat. Snapper, mahi mahi, trout, or grouper would also work well as the base for these tacos.

Servings: 4 • **Prep time:** 25 mins. • **Cook time:** 15 mins.

Ingredients
- Cucumber Slaw (top right)
- Basil Pico de Gallo (bottom right)
- 1 pound fresh black drum, filet
- ¼ cup olive oil
- Sea salt and pepper, to taste
- Serve with 4 corn-and-flour-blend tortillas

1. First prepare the cucumber slaw and basil pico de gallo (see recipes) to allow their flavors to develop while you prepare the fish. Preheat the grill.
2. Brush the fish with the olive oil and season it liberally with sea salt and pepper. Place the fish in a grill basket. Grill it over low, indirect heat for 3–4 minutes per side. Serve with the tortillas, cucumber slaw, and basil pico de gallo

Cucumber Slaw

Ingredients
- 1 cucumber, grated
- ¼ sweet bell pepper, grated
- 1 tablespoon rice vinegar
- 2 teaspoons sugar
- Large pinch of salt

1. Combine all of the ingredients in a medium bowl and let it rest for at least 15 minutes, to allow its flavors to develop.

Basil Pico de Gallo

Ingredients
- 1 cup sweet cherry tomatoes, diced
- 1–2 jalapeños, seeded and minced
- ½ cup 1015 (or other sweet) onion, diced
- 1 tablespoon lime juice
- 1 clove garlic, minced
- 1 small bunch basil, chopped

1. Combine all of the ingredients in a medium bowl. Let rest for at least 15 minutes to allow its flavors to develop.

Berry Skillet Crisp

Warning: You may need to double this recipe due to high demand. Serve this berry crisp (you pick the best berries) warm out of the oven, topped with scoops of vanilla ice cream and big spoons.

Servings: 6 • **Prep time:** 3 mins. • **Cook time:** 20 mins.

Ingredients
For the berry mix
- 2 pints fresh berries (I recommend raspberries)
- 2 tablespoons sugar
- 1 tablespoon all-purpose flour
- Juice of 1 lemon

For the topping
- ½ cup flour
- ½ cup rolled oats
- ½ cup brown sugar
- 4 tablespoons butter

1. Preheat oven to 350°F. In a medium bowl, combine the topping ingredients with your fingers or a pastry blender until incorporated into pea-sized crumbles.
2. Heat two small cast-iron skillets (I recommend 6-inch diameter) over medium heat. Add 1 pint of berries to each skillet, and stir in the sugar, flour, and lemon until well incorporated.
3. Stirring occasionally, cook until the berries have reduced and a sauce has formed, about 5–7 minutes. Spoon the topping onto both of the berry mixtures and bake for 10–15 minutes, until the crust is golden brown. Serve the crisps warm, right out of the skillet.

Berry Dutch Baby

Known by many names (including, but not limited to, "hootenanny" and "Dutch Puff"), "Dutch baby pancakes" is something of a misnomer. Dutch babies are more closely akin to popovers or Yorkshire puddings—they are cooked in the oven and leavened by agitated eggs.

Servings: 6 • **Prep time:** 10 mins. • **Cook time:** 25 mins.

Ingredients
For the pancake batter
- ¾ cup all-purpose flour
- 3 eggs
- 1 tablespoon granulated sugar
- ½ teaspoon salt
- Zest of 1 lemon
- 3 tablespoons butter
- ¾ cup whole milk
- 1 teaspoon vanilla extract

For the berry syrup
- ½ pint fresh berries, cleaned with stems removed
- 2 tablespoons sugar
- 2 tablespoons water
- Juice of one lemon

1. Preheat the oven to 400°F. Place a 9-inch cast-iron skillet in the oven as it preheats.
2. In a blender or food processor, combine the flour, eggs, sugar, milk, vanilla, salt, and lemon zest, blending until smooth. Add the butter to the preheated skillet and swirl to coat the surface evenly. Pour in the prepared batter and close the oven quickly to retain as much heat as possible. Bake for 20 minutes, until the batter is golden brown and puffed in the center.
3. While the pancake cooks, place a small saucepan over medium heat. Add the ingredients for the berry syrup and cook for 3–5 minutes, or until the desired consistency is reached.
4. To serve, ladle the berry syrup over the pancake and sift confectioner's sugar over the top.

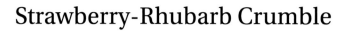

Strawberry-Rhubarb Crumble

Much of my focus in the kitchen is devoted to saving my most precious resource: time. Many of my recipes have minimal active time, and instead let the ingredients or the oven do most of the work. This crumble is no exception. Strawberry and rhubarb create their own syrup while languishing in sugar (while you languish on the couch).

Makes: one 8 x 8-inch pan • **Prep time:** 10 mins.
• **Inactive prep time:** 15 mins. • **Cook time:** 50 mins.

Ingredients
For the fruit filling
- 2 cups rhubarb, diced
- 2 cups strawberries, chopped
- ⅔ cup sugar
- ¼ teaspoon salt
- ¼ cup all-purpose flour
- 1 tablespoon butter, melted
- 1 teaspoon vanilla extract

For the crumble topping
- 1½ cups all-purpose flour
- 1 cup brown sugar
- ½ teaspoons cinnamon
- ¼ teaspoons nutmeg
- ¼ teaspoon salt
- ½ cup butter, cubed
- Serve with vanilla ice cream

1. Preheat the oven to 350°F. Combine the rhubarb, strawberries, and sugar in a large bowl and let it sit for 15 minutes, stirring occasionally. Sprinkle the salt and flour onto the rhubarb mixture before adding the butter and vanilla. Mix well until the rhubarb and berries are coated and the flour has dissolved. Transfer it to an 8 x 8-inch baking dish.
2. To make the crumble, whisk the flour, brown sugar, cinnamon, nutmeg, and salt together in a medium bowl. Using a fork or a pastry blender, cut in the butter until the mixture resembles oatmeal. Distribute the crumble topping evenly over the prepared filling.
3. Bake the crumble in the oven for 50 minutes, until the filling is bubbly and the topping is golden brown. Check crumble at 35 minutes and, if the outer edge of the topping is already browned, cover it with aluminum foil. Serve warm with vanilla ice cream.

Tomato Galette

Savory tomato pie makes a lovely Sunday brunch entree. Dehydrating the tomatoes with a treatment of salt prevents the pie from becoming soggy. Try substituting zucchini, corn, eggplant, or tender greens when your tomatoes stop setting fruit for an equally delicious treat.

Makes: 1 large pie • **Prep time:** 30 mins. • **Cook time:** 60 mins.

Ingredients
For the dough
- 2 cups all-purpose flour
- 1½ teaspoons salt
- ¾ teaspoon dried basil
- ½ teaspoon garlic powder
- ¾ cup (1½ sticks) unsalted butter, cubed
- ⅓ cup ice cold water

For the filling
- 1 pound tomatoes, sliced into ⅓-inch slices
- 1 teaspoon salt, plus ½ teaspoon
- 8 ounces mascarpone
- ¼ cup olive oil
- 2 tablespoons fresh basil, chopped
- 2 tablespoons fresh mint, chopped
- 5 garlic cloves, minced
- ¼ teaspoons black pepper
- 1 egg, beaten

1. Preheat the oven to 400°F. To get the filling started, lay the tomato slices in a single layer on a surface covered with paper towels. Sprinkle the tomatoes with salt. Let them sit while you move on to the dough.
2. To make the dough, add the flour, salt, basil, and garlic powder to a food processor and pulse for 30 seconds, until well mixed. Add the butter and pulse for 10 seconds. Add the ice water and blend for 10 seconds until a soft dough forms. Roll the dough into a large circle, about 16 inches in diameter. Transfer the dough round to a baking sheet lined with parchment paper.
3. To continue preparing the filling, blot the tomatoes with paper towels to remove any moisture that has accumulated. In a medium bowl, combine the mascarpone, olive oil, basil, mint, garlic, ½ teaspoon of salt, and pepper. Spread the cheese mixture evenly across the dough round, leaving a 1½-inch border all the way around.
4. Top the cheese with the tomatoes and fold the edge of the dough over the tomatoes, pleating the dough as you work around the pie. Brush the crust with the egg wash and bake for 60 minutes, until the crust is golden brown.

Gazpacho

Not a summer goes by that I don't make a big batch of gazpacho. Few dishes are as cooling or invigorating in 100-degree (or hotter) weather ... and don't get me started on the humidity!

Servings: 8–12 • **Prep time:** 7 mins.

Ingredients

- 2 pounds tomatoes
- 3 cups watermelon
- 1 cucumber, peeled
- 1 white onion, peeled and stems removed
- 4 cloves garlic, peeled
- 1 jalapeño, seeded and pith removed
- 1 teaspoon salt
- ½ teaspoon cayenne pepper
- ½ cup champagne, or sherry vinegar
- ½ cup extra-virgin olive oil
- ½ cup fresh basil, packed

1. Combine the vegetables in a large blender or food processor. Blend until smooth (or for chunkier gazpacho, only pulse 3 times for about 2–3 seconds each).
2. Add in the remaining ingredients. (I recommend starting with half the salt and vinegar, and working your way to the full measure, or to taste.) Serve right away in a chilled bowl or shot glasses.

Chèvre-Stuffed Squash Blossoms

At the height of our farmer's market rounds, my husband and I made fast friends with a neighboring vendor that sold goat cheese of such quality and freshness, nothing at the grocer could touch it. Years later, their goat cheese is commercially available and regionally known as the best around. If you ever make it to South Texas, try any and every cheese from Thompson's Dairy Farms. And yes, maybe even perform some yoga stretches with their baby goats.

Servings: 4–6 • **Prep time:** 10 mins. • **Cook time:** 6 mins.

Ingredients

- 3 cups cooking oil with a high smoke point
- 1 cup chèvre
- 2 tablespoons fresh basil, chopped
- 2 tablespoons oregano, chopped
- ¼ teaspoons red pepper flakes
- 12 large squash blossoms
- ½ cup all-purpose flour
- ½ teaspoon kosher salt
- ½ cup sparkling water, plus 2 tablespoons
- 1 tablespoon Parmigiano Reggiano, shredded

1. Place the oil in a large pan over medium-high heat. In a small bowl, combine the chèvre, herbs, and pepper flakes. Carefully open and fill each squash blossom with a tablespoon of the chèvre mixture.
2. In a shallow dish, combine the flour, salt, and sparkling water to form a batter. Twist the end of each filled squash blossom and, holding on to the stem, immerse them in the batter. Add them carefully to the hot oil, using caution not to crowd the pan. Fry each stuffed blossom for about 1 minute, then carefully turn them and cook 1 minute on the opposite side. Transfer the blossoms to a paper towel–lined plate and sprinkle the Parmigiano Reggiano on top prior to serving.

Green Beans with Miso Dressing

All busy weeknight dishes should be this easy, satisfying, and time-conserving. Try not putting this miso dressing on everything. No, seriously, I literally can't stop.

Servings: 6–8 • **Prep time:** 3 mins. • **Cook time:** 6–8 mins.

Ingredients

- 2 tablespoons avocado or peanut oil
- 2 pounds green beans
- 1 tablespoon sesame oil
- 3 cloves garlic, minced
- 1 tablespoon miso
- 1 teaspoon honey
- Garnishes: 2 scallions, thinly sliced; sesame seeds

1. In a wok or sauté pan, heat the oil over medium-high heat. Once the oil begins to shimmer, add the green beans and cook for 5 minutes, stirring frequently.
2. Meanwhile, combine the sesame oil, garlic, miso, and honey in a small bowl. Drizzle the dressing over the beans and cook for 1–2 minutes. Garnish the coated green beans with scallions and sesame seeds before serving.

Dark Chocolate Zucchini Bread

"What am I supposed to do with all these zucchini?!" is a common refrain heard in my kitchen come July. Dark chocolate zucchini bread checks so many boxes: it's a great way to use zucchini, it's exceptionally moist and tender, and it crushes any chocolate craving.

Makes: 1 loaf • **Prep time:** 7 mins. • **Cooking time:** 45 mins.

Ingredients

- 2 medium zucchinis
- ¾ cup brown sugar
- ¼ cup olive oil
- ¼ cup plain yogurt
- 2 eggs

- 1 teaspoon vanilla
- 1 cup all-purpose flour
- ½ cup dark cocoa/cacao powder
- ½ teaspoon salt

- ½ teaspoon baking powder
- ½ teaspoon baking soda
- 1 cup dark chocolate chips (at least 60% cacao)

1. Preheat the oven to 350°F. Spray a loaf pan (8 x 4 x 2½ inches) with nonstick cooking spray.
2. Remove the ends from the zucchini and grate it over a colander. Using the back of a large spoon or spatula, press the zucchini against the colander to remove excess fluid.
3. Transfer the grated zucchini to a clean bowl. Add the brown sugar, olive oil, yogurt, eggs, and vanilla, mixing until combined.
4. In a separate bowl, combine the dry ingredients. Mix the wet and dry ingredients together until just combined. Fold in ½ cup of chocolate chips.
5. Transfer the batter to prepared loaf pan. Top with the remaining chocolate chips. Bake for 45 minutes, until a toothpick inserted into the center of the loaf comes out clean.

Summer Salad

My husband I spent our honeymoon in Greece. We loved the ancient ruins, beautiful beaches, and the salads (and the salads were a very close third, by the way). This summer salad closely mirrors my favorite Grecian salad, minus the sweet Nona in the kitchen and the house-made wine.

Servings: 6–8 • **Prep time:** 20–25 mins.

Ingredients
For the quick-pickled peppers
- 6–10 banana peppers, thinly sliced
- ¼ cup distilled white vinegar
- 1 tablespoon white wine vinegar
- ¼ cup water
- ¼ teaspoon sea salt

For the salad
- 2 pounds vine-ripened tomatoes, cut into chunks
- 1 cucumber, chopped
- 2 avocados, chopped
- ½ sweet onion, sliced thinly
- ½ cup fresh basil, chiffonade
- 6 ounces goat or feta cheese

For the grapefruit vinaigrette
- 2 tablespoons freshly squeezed grapefruit juice
- 2 tablespoons balsamic vinegar
- ½ cup extra-virgin olive oil
- 2 tablespoons sweet onion, grated
- ¼ cup fresh basil, packed
- ¼ teaspoon sea salt
- Black pepper, to taste

1. To make the quick-pickled peppers, combine all the ingredients in a small bowl and let it sit for 30 minutes. Meanwhile, to begin making the salad, combine the tomatoes, cucumber, avocados, onion, and basil in a large bowl.
2. To make the grapefruit vinaigrette, combine all the ingredients in a food processor or blender and pulse until completely combined. Pour the vinaigrette over the tomato mixture and toss to combine. Top the salad with the pickled peppers and cheese before serving.

Kofta Kabobs with Tzatziki

Kofta is a simple preparation of ground meat with herbs and spices. One simply cannot serve kofta without tzatziki—the bright flavors of the cucumber, garlic, and dill in creamy yogurt temper the grilled meat.

Servings: 6 • **Prep time:** 15 mins. • **Cook time:** 15 mins.

Ingredients

For the kabobs

- 1 pound grass-fed ground beef
- 4 cloves garlic, minced
- ½ onion, minced
- 3 tablespoons fresh parsley, chopped
- 3 tablespoons fresh mint, chopped
- ½ teaspoon cumin
- ¼ teaspoon cinnamon
- 1 teaspoon kosher salt
- ½ teaspoon cayenne

For the tzatziki

- ½ cucumber, grated
- 1 cup Greek yogurt
- 2 tablespoons fresh dill, chopped
- 2 tablespoons extra-virgin olive oil
- 1 clove garlic, grated
- Juice of 1 lemon
- ½ teaspoon fine sea salt
- ¼ teaspoon freshly cracked black pepper

1. Preheat the grill according to the manufacturer's instructions. Submerge 8 wooden skewers in water for at least 10 minutes.
2. To make the kabobs, combine all the ingredients in a large bowl and mix well with your hands or a wooden spoon. Divide the kabob mixture into 8 portions. Using your hands, shape the meat around one of the pre-soaked skewers. Repeat for the rest of the meat portions using the remaining skewers.
3. With the grill lid open, cook each skewer on direct heat for 2 minutes on each side. Move the skewers to indirect heat and cook for 10–12 minutes, with the grill lid closed, until the internal temperature reaches 160°F. Transfer the kabobs to a platter and let the kabobs rest while you prepare the tzatziki.
4. To make the tzatziki, strain the grated cucumber in a fine mesh sieve by firmly pressing a spoon against the flesh to remove excess moisture. (Alternatively, wrap the grated cucumber in a paper towel and twist the paper towel, applying pressure to squeeze out the juices.) Transfer the grated cucumber to a medium bowl and add in the remaining ingredients. Stir the mixture well. Serve the kabobs with tzatziki on the side, or build a gyro using the pita bread recipe on page 126.

Greek Buddha Bowl

Buddha bowls gained popularity as meatless meals after being featured in an issue of *Martha Stewart Living* in the 1990s. The combination of complex carbs, lean protein, and healthy fats makes for a delicious take-along lunch, right from the Mediterranean.

Makes: 1 large bowl • **Prep time:** 7 mins. • **Cook time:** 20 mins.

Ingredients
For the tabbouleh
- ½ cup quinoa
- 2 tablespoons parsley, chopped
- Juice of 1 lemon
- 1 tablespoon olive oil
- Salt and pepper, to taste

For the Buddha bowl
- 1 cup fresh spinach
- ½ cup garbanzo beans (or chickpeas), drained and rinsed
- ⅓ cucumber, sliced
- 2 ounces crumbled feta
- 2 roasted red peppers, chopped
- 2 ounces Kalamata olives, pitted
- 5 cherry tomatoes, halved
- 2 tablespoons olive oil
- 1 tablespoon red wine vinegar
- Fresh oregano, chopped

1. Heat 1 cup of water on medium-high in a medium saucepan. Add the quinoa and cook uncovered, stirring occasionally, until all the liquid has been absorbed and the quinoa has swelled. Remove the pan from heat and cover, letting it steam for 5 minutes. Add the parsley, lemon juice, olive oil, salt, and pepper, mixing well to combine.
2. In a large bowl or storage container (with 2-cup capacity), assemble the bowl by adding the tabbouleh, spinach, garbanzo beans, cucumber, feta, red peppers, olives, and tomatoes. Top the Buddha bowl with the olive oil, red wine vinegar, fresh oregano, and salt and pepper. Refrigerate until ready to enjoy.

Southern-Style Black-Eyed Peas

Every New Year's Eve my mom would eye me until I choked down a spoonful of canned black-eyed peas. To this day, there is little I find redeeming about most black-eyed pea dishes, which usually start with a store-bought can—but these peas are different. Fresh black-eyed peas are a game-changer!

Servings: 8 • **Prep time:** 10 mins. • **Inactive prep time:** 8 hrs. • **Cooking time:** 1 hr.

Ingredients

- 1 pound fresh black-eyed peas
- ½ pound fresh bacon, chopped
- 1 medium onion, diced
- 4 garlic cloves, minced
- 1 tablespoon cayenne pepper sauce
- 4 cups chicken or vegetable stock
- 2 bay leaves
- 1½ cups fresh cilantro, chopped
- Salt and pepper, to taste

1. Rinse and drain the peas and remove any undesirable pieces.
2. Place ½ of the chopped bacon into a medium pot over medium heat. Brown the bacon until the desired crispness is achieved. Remove the bacon and set aside on a paper towel–lined plate, add the onion along with the remaining bacon, and cook for 3–5 minutes. Add the garlic and cook for 1 minute.
3. Add the cayenne pepper sauce and the peas, stirring until the peas are coated. Add the stock and bay leaves and bring the mixture to a boil. Reduce the heat, cover the pot, and simmer for approximately 30 minutes. Remove the bay leaves, add the cilantro, and season to taste. Serve topped with the crisp bacon. Garnish with bay leaves, if desired.

Campfire-Skewered Okra

Perfect for a camping weekend or a Saturday around the fire, you'll come back to this recipe year after year during okra season.

Servings: 4 • **Prep time:** 3 mins. • **Cook time:** 20 mins.

Ingredients
- Avocado oil, as needed
- 1 pound fresh okra
- Salt and pepper, to taste

1. Drizzle the oil over the okra and season it with salt and pepper. Prepare a sturdy stick by removing the smaller twigs near the end. In the thickest part of each okra, skewer with the prepared stick, coat the okra with cooking oil, and season to taste with salt and pepper.
2. Roast the okra over the fire for 10 minutes on each side, or until it begins to turn golden brown and is heated through.

Cucumber-Lime Popsicles

Gather the kiddies for this summer treat. Who am I kidding, once they try them, you won't be able to get them out of the kitchen. They're as fun to make as they are to eat.

Makes: 8 popsicles • **Prep time:** 5 mins. • **Inactive prep time:** 4 hrs.

Ingredients:

- 3 cups freshly squeezed lime juice
- 1 cup sugar
- 4 sprigs rosemary, cut into 3-inch lengths
- 4 sprigs mint, cut into 3-inch lengths
- 1 lime or lemon, thinly sliced
- ½ cucumber, thinly sliced

1. In a saucepan, heat the lime juice and sugar over medium low. Whisk until the sugar has dissolved.
2. Using popsicle molds, fill each individual popsicle mold half full with the limeade. Add a sprig of rosemary or mint to the center of each mold. Place a slice of lemon, lime, cucumber, or other fresh fruit on either side of each herb. There should be 2 slices of fresh fruit for each mold. Top off each mold with the remaining limeade.
3. Freeze the popsicles for about 4 hours, or until they are completely set. Prior to serving, place the molds under warm running water for about 10 seconds to help release the popsicles.

Fresh Fruit Pops

Paletas, Mexican ice pops, are a summer staple where I live. Ice cream trucks hand out dulce de leche, mango, and piña popsicles to sweaty children taking a break from touch football. The fruteria on the corner has a deep freezer full of them. Enjoy experimenting with fruit, sweetened milk, chocolate, or other flavors.

Makes: 8 popsicles • **Prep time:** 5 mins. • **Inactive prep time:** 4 hrs.

Ingredients
For tropical pops
- 2 cups fresh pineapple, peeled
- 1 can coconut milk
- ⅓ cup shredded coconut

For strawberry banana pops
- 4 bananas, peeled
- 2 cups strawberries, washed, with tops removed, plus 3 strawberries, sliced lengthwise

1. Blend the fresh fruit (and coconut milk if using) in a blender on high until the mixture is completely smooth. Stir in the shredded coconut for tropical pops or add strawberry slices for the strawberry banana pops.
2. Freeze for at least 4 hours. Prior to serving, place the molds under warm running water for about 10 seconds to help release the popsicles.

Burrata with Grilled Tomatoes and Peaches

Even if you're not big on cheese (that's a conversation for another time), the creamy, delicate flavor of burrata may change your mind. Round, spongy mozzarella gives way to buttery cream, which mixes with the olive oil and vinegar to create a velvety sauce for the grilled fruit.

Servings: 2–4 • **Prep time:** 2 mins. • **Cook time:** 15–20 mins.

Ingredients

- 1 pound peaches, each sliced into 8 pieces
- 1 pound tomatoes, each sliced into 8 pieces
- 2 tablespoons peanut or avocado oil
- ½ teaspoon salt, plus more to taste
- ¼ teaspoon cracked black pepper, plus more to taste
- 1 serving burrata
- 2 tablespoons olive oil
- 1 tablespoon balsamic vinegar

1. Preheat the grill to medium-high (400°F). Brush the peaches and tomatoes with the oil and season them with salt and pepper. Place the fruits on the grill, with 1–2 inches of space between them. Grill them for 3–4 minutes on each side, until well-defined grill marks appear.
2. Transfer the grilled fruits to a large bowl or platter and ring them around the fresh burrata. Drizzle the olive oil and balsamic vinegar over the fruits and cheese. Finish with extra salt and pepper, to taste.

Plum Upside-Down Cake

Many of my friends and acquaintances have started cutting out gluten from their diets and have seen a notable reduction in joint pain, gastrointestinal upset, fatigue, and symptoms of leaky gut. Move before "Many of my friends..." to make this the first sentence.

Makes: 1 single-layer 9-inch cake • **Prep time:** 10 mins. • **Cook time:** 40 mins.

Ingredients

- ½ cup brown sugar
- 4 tablespoons (½ stick) unsalted butter, melted, plus ½ cup (1 stick) butter, softened
- 3 large plums, sliced into ⅛-inch segments
- 1½ cups almond flour
- 1 cup granulated sugar
- ½ cup yogurt
- Pinch of salt
- 3 eggs
- 1 tablespoon orange zest
- 2 teaspoons vanilla
- 2 teaspoons baking powder
- ½ teaspoon almond extract

1. Preheat the oven to 375°F. Oil a 9-inch cake pan.
2. Mix the brown sugar and melted butter in a small bowl. Pour the sugar-and-butter mixture into the cake pan and spread it evenly to coat the bottom. Layer the plum segments on top of the mixture until the entire surface is covered.
3. Combine the remaining ingredients together in a large bowl. Whisk until the mixture is smooth. Pour the cake batter into the cake pan, completely covering the layered plum slices.
4. Bake the cake for 40 minutes, or until a toothpick inserted into the center comes out clean. Cool the cake on a rack to room temperature.
5. Once the cake has cooled, place a large plate or platter on top of the cake pan. Invert the pan in one fluid motion, so that the cake dislodges onto the plate, displaying a lovely, plum-covered surface.

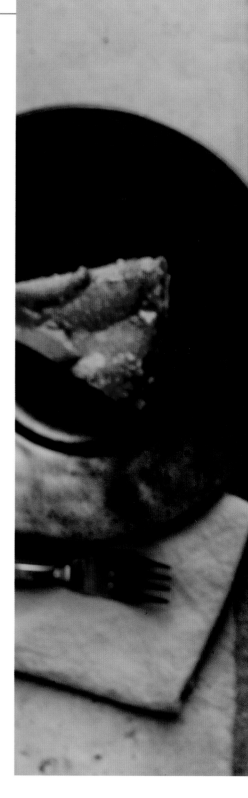

Tempura Veggies

Some recipes for tempura vegetables recommend soaking starchy vegetables in water to remove excess starch. For a crisp batter, traditional Japanese methods insist on stirring with chopsticks to prevent overmixing. The temperature difference between the cold batter and hot oil also ensures an extra-crispy final product.

Servings: 4 • **Prep time:** 10 mins. • **Cook time:** 20 mins.

Ingredients
For the vegetable tempura

- 2 pounds assorted vegetables (green beans, mushrooms, onions, sweet potatoes, squash, or eggplant)
- 4 cups peanut, canola, or vegetable oil
- ¾ cup all-purpose flour
- ¼ cup rice flour
- ½ cup corn or arrowroot starch
- ½ teaspoon fine salt
- 1 egg
- ¾ cup ice-cold carbonated water

For the dipping sauce

- ¼ cup mirin
- ¼ cup soy sauce
- 1 tablespoon maple syrup
- 1 tablespoon sesame oil

1. Prepare the vegetables by washing them thoroughly and removing any tough skins and stems. Dry the vegetables with a towel or paper towels to remove excess moisture.
2. In a deep-rimmed pan, preheat the oil to 350°F. Whisk the flours, starch, and salt together in a big bowl. Place the bowl of dry ingredients over a bowl of ice water to keep it cool. Add the egg and carbonated water to the flour mixture and mix for 20 seconds.
3. Dip the vegetables in the batter then fry them for 3–4 minutes on each side. Make sure not to overcrowd the pan by using only half the surface area of the oil. Transfer the fried vegetables to a cooling rack. Continue to fry the vegetables in this manner until they have all been fried.
4. Combine the ingredients for the dipping sauce in a small bowl and serve with the tempura vegetables.

Spaghetti Zoodles with Sesame Ginger Dressing

Few of us need another kitchen gadget crowding our cabinets. My arguments in favor of purchasing a spiralizer are that they're inexpensive, easy to use, don't take up much space, and you can spiral up almost any large fruit or vegetable. The best news: prepared zucchini noodles are now stocked at most local grocers.

Servings: 2 • **Prep time:** 5 mins.

Ingredients

- ½ cup tahini
- ¼ cup nut butter
- ¼ cup soy sauce or liquid aminos
- 1 tablespoon sesame oil
- 1 tablespoon rice wine vinegar
- 1 tablespoon honey
- 2 teaspoons ginger, grated
- 2 cups spiralized zucchini (zucchini noodles, aka zoodles)
- Garnishes: gochugaru, sesame seeds, toasted nuts

1. In a medium bowl, whisk together the tahini, nut butter, soy sauce, sesame oil, rice wine vinegar, honey, and ginger until smooth.
2. Place the zoodles in a serving bowl and drizzle the sesame ginger dressing over top. Garnish with gochugaru, sesame seeds, and toasted nuts and serve.

Five Variations on Hummus

Hummus is best known as a dip for pita bread and vegetables, but it's also a great healthy option for adding flavor to sandwiches, wraps, and salads. My fresh chickpea hummus variation is more traditional, but the sky is the limit for this versatile snack.

Makes: 6 appetizer portions
- **Prep time:** 15 mins.
- **Cook time:** 25–45 mins.

Beet Hummus

Ingredients

- 3 beets, scrubbed, with tops removed
- 1 teaspoon salt
- Pepper, to taste
- ⅓ cup olive oil
- 8 ounces chickpeas
- ½ cup fresh cilantro, parsley, or dill
- 2 cloves garlic
- ⅓ cup tahini
- Juice of 1 lemon
- 1 teaspoon za'atar
- Serve with crudité, crackers, or bread

1. Preheat the oven to 375°F. Season the beets with salt and pepper and coat them with olive oil. Roast the beets until they are fork tender, about 35 minutes. Remove them from the oven and let them cool.
2. Meanwhile, combine the remaining ingredients in a blender or food processor. Add the beets once they are cool enough to handle. Blend the mixture on high, scraping down the sides on occasion, for about 5 minutes, until it reaches a creamy, smooth texture. Serve with crudité, crackers, or bread.

Sweet Potato Hummus

Ingredients

- 2 sweet potatoes
- 8 ounces chickpeas, shelled
- 2 cloves garlic
- ⅓ cup olive oil
- ⅓ cup tahini
- Juice of 1 lemon
- ½ teaspoon smoked paprika
- ½ teaspoon chipotle
- ¼ teaspoon cumin
- Serve with crudité, crackers, or bread

1. Roast the sweet potatoes for 45 minutes at 400°F.
2. Remove the potatoes from the oven and spoon out the flesh into a blender or food processor. Add the remaining ingredients. Puree until smooth and serve.

Black Bean Hummus

Ingredients

- 16 ounces black beans, shelled
- 2 cloves garlic
- ⅓ cup olive oil
- ⅓ cup tahini
- 2 tablespoons lime juice
- ¼ cup fresh cilantro
- ½ teaspoon cumin
- Salt, to taste
- Serve with crudité, crackers, or bread

1. Add black beans to a pot of salted, boiling water and cook for 3 minutes, or until the beans are tender.
2. Strain the beans and place them in a food processor, along with remaining ingredients. Puree until it is smooth and serve.

Fresh Chickpea Hummus

Ingredients

- 16 ounces chickpeas, shelled
- 2 cloves garlic
- ⅓ cup olive oil
- ⅓ cup tahini
- Juice of 1 lemon
- 1 teaspoon za'atar
- 1 teaspoon salt
- ½ teaspoon cumin
- Serve with crudité, crackers, or bread

1. Add chickpeas to a pot of salted, boiling water. Boil for 2–3 minutes, or until the chickpeas are tender.
2. Strain the chickpeas and place them in a food processor, along with remaining ingredients. Puree until smooth and serve.

Butternut Squash Hummus

Ingredients

- 1 butternut squash
- ½ cup parsley
- 2 cloves garlic
- ⅓ cup olive oil
- ⅓ cup tahini
- Juice of 1 lemon
- Salt, to taste
- ¼ teaspoon smoked paprika
- ¼ teaspoon cinnamon
- ½ teaspoon cumin
- Serve with crudité, crackers, or bread

1. Slice butternut squash in half and spoon out its seeds and pith. Roast it, cut side down, for 45 minutes at 375°F.
2. Spoon the roasted squash into your food processor, along with remaining ingredients. Puree until it is smooth and serve.

Fall

As summer gives way to fall, pumpkins and winter squash finally begin to wither at the stem, their skins thicken and become impenetrable even to the most determined fingernail, their color evolves, just like the tree leaves that provide fall's beautiful colors.

Fall may be my favorite time in the garden. Carrots, radishes, and parsnips are ready without too much fuss. We like to densely plant them once summer has sizzled, intersperse them with dill and coriander, then thin them throughout the season. Their greens and immature fruits make for a refreshing addition to any fall soup.

Houseguests will often find a Kabocha or Hubbard squash hiding under our guest bed. We don't have cellars in the shifting sands of our small coastal town, so these air-conditioned quarters will have to do. Instead, we have a longer window for the fruits of fall. With hectic school and work schedules, I opt for easier one-pot meals that don't skimp on flavor. You'll find warming food from dishes I've adapted from around the world.

Fall is the time for harvesting comfort food staples and making warm dishes to brighten the cool nights.

In Season

Apples
Bananas
Beets
Bell peppers
Broccoli
Brussels sprouts
Cabbage
Carrots
Cauliflower
Celery
Collard greens
Cranberries
Garlic
Ginger

Grapes
Green beans
Kale
Kiwi
Lemons
Lettuce
Limes
Mangos
Mushrooms
Onions
Parsnips
Pears
Peas
Pineapples

Potatoes
Pumpkins
Radishes
Raspberries
Rutabagas
Spinach
Sweet potatoes
Swiss chard
Turnips
Winter squash
Yams

Skillet Chicken and Rice

Every modern culture has developed their own take on chicken and rice over time. My adaptation requires little prep time and even less time in the kitchen doing dishes afterward.

Servings: 4–6 • **Prep time:** 5 mins. • **Cooking time:** 1 hr.

Ingredients

- 2 tablespoons olive oil, plus 2 more tablespoons
- 1 large onion, sliced
- 2 sweet peppers, seeded and sliced
- 1 bone-in whole chicken with skin on, broken down into parts
- 1 teaspoon paprika
- ¾ teaspoon cumin
- ¼ teaspoon cayenne
- 1–2 teaspoons salt
- 5 sprigs tarragon (or ½ teaspoon dried tarragon)
- 4 cloves garlic, minced
- 1 cup uncooked basmati rice
- 2–2¼ cups chicken broth or stock
- 2 bay leaves
- Juice of 1 lime, to taste

1. Preheat the oven to 375°F. Heat a large cast-iron skillet over medium-high heat. Once you are only able to hold your hand over the skillet for less than 3 seconds, add the olive oil, onion, and peppers. Cook for about 5 minutes and set the onions and peppers aside on a clean plate. Return the skillet to the heat.
2. Season the chicken with paprika, cumin, cayenne, and salt. Add additional olive oil to the skillet, and, cooking in batches to avoid crowding, cook the chicken for 6–7 minutes on each side. (Add tarragon at this time if you're using dried tarragon.) Set the chicken aside.
3. Add the garlic and rice to the skillet and cook for 1 minute, stirring frequently. Add the chicken broth and reduce the heat to low. Simmer the rice for 10 minutes, until most of the liquid is absorbed. If necessary, add additional broth. Return the onion, peppers, and chicken back to skillet, along with the bay leaves and fresh tarragon (if using). Cover with an oven-proof lid or aluminum foil.
4. Place the skillet in the oven and cook for 30–40 minutes, until the juices from the chicken run clear. Remove the bay leaves. Squeeze the lime over the chicken and rice and serve.

Baba Ghanoush with Pita Bread

Originating from Lebanon, baba ghanoush is eggplant at its finest. Grilling helps tame the compounds that give eggplant its bitter taste. Alternatively, you can roast the eggplant slices for 30 minutes at 400°F.

Servings: 6 • **Prep time:** 7 mins. • **Cook time:** 20 mins. • **Inactive prep time:** 10 mins.

Ingredients
- 1 large eggplant, thickly sliced
- ¼ cup tahini
- 2 cloves garlic
- 2 tablespoons fresh parsley
- 1 tablespoon good-quality extra-virgin olive oil, plus more to taste
- ¼ teaspoon salt
- Juice of 1 lemon
- Pinch of cumin
- Serve with Pita Bread (see recipe below)

1. Preheat the grill. Drizzle olive oil over the eggplant. Grill eggplant slices on direct heat for 2 minutes on each side, then move them to indirect heat with the grill lid closed for 10–15 minutes, or until the flesh is tender.
2. Remove the eggplant slices from the grill. Once they have cooled, remove the peels. Place the eggplant pulp and remaining ingredients in a food processor and pulse until smooth, about 45 seconds. Serve with pita bread.

Pita Bread

Servings: 8 • **Prep time:** 7 mins. • **Inactive prep time:** 1 hr. • **Cook time:** 10 mins.

Ingredients
- 1 packet (2¼ teaspoons) fast-acting dry yeast
- 1½ teaspoons sugar
- 1⅓ cups water
- 4 cups bread flour
- 1 tablespoon salt
- ¼ cup olive oil

1. Mix the yeast, sugar, and water in a large mixing bowl. Let it sit for 5 minutes, until bubbles begin to form. Add the remaining ingredients and knead for 5 minutes, until a smooth, elastic dough is formed. Let it rise for 1 hour.
2. Place a cast-iron skillet on medium-high heat. Divide the dough into 8 equal pieces and form them into balls. Using a rolling pin, roll out each dough ball until it is ⅛ inch thick. Cook the pitas on the preheated skillet for 2 minutes on each side. Serve warm alongside your dish of choice.

Baba ghanoush and pita bread are the perfect companions to some delicious kofta kabobs (see page 106).

Chicken Mole Poblano

Mole poblano is a traditional Mexican preparation known for its intensity in flavor and the time required. This version is more efficient than some, while retaining the traditional flavor and intent—a complexity of peppers, tomatillos, and nutty chocolate.

Servings: 4–6 • **Prep time:** 30 mins. • **Cooking time:** 1 hr. 30 mins.

Ingredients
For the chicken

- 3–5 pounds whole chicken, skin on
- 2–3 tablespoons olive oil
- Salt and pepper, to taste

For the mole poblano

- 8 ancho peppers, stems removed, seeds reserved
- 4 pasilla peppers, stems removed, seeds reserved
- 5 guajillo peppers, stems removed, seeds reserved
- 1 cup lard
- 1 sweet onion, chopped
- 6 tomatillos, coarsely chopped
- 4 cloves garlic, minced
- ¾ cup raw, unsalted nuts (pecans, hazelnuts, almonds, or to your preference)
- ¼ cup raw pumpkin seeds
- 2 ounces sesame seeds
- ½ teaspoon anise seeds
- ½ teaspoon cumin seeds
- 1 cinnamon stick (canela)
- ½ teaspoon black peppercorns
- 2 corn tortillas, torn into pieces
- 2 French rolls (bolillos), 2–3 days old, torn into pieces
- ¼ cup raisins
- 5 cups low-sodium chicken broth
- 1½ ounces Mexican chocolate, chopped (or dark, bittersweet chocolate)
- 2 tablespoons sugar
- Salt, to taste

1. To prepare the chicken, preheat the oven with a roasting pan inside to 375°F. Brush the olive oil on the chicken and season generously with salt and pepper. Place the chicken on the roasting pan, breast side up. Cook for 30 minutes.
2. Flip the chicken so that its backbone is facing up. Cook for 30 minutes. Check to ensure the internal temperature of the meatiest part of one leg has reached 165°F. If the chicken is not yet hot enough, rotate it so that it is breast side up, and return it to the oven for up to 30 minutes, or until the proper internal temperature is reached.
3. Let the chicken rest for 10–15 minutes.
4. To prepare the mole poblano, while the oven preheats, place the peppers in a large cast-iron skillet over high heat. Roast the peppers for 2 minutes on each side, until the skin starts to brown and the peppers become fragrant. Remove the peppers from the skillet and place them in a large bowl with hot water. Let the peppers reconstitute for 10 minutes and set them aside.

5. Heat ½ cup lard in a skillet over medium heat. Add the onion, tomatillos, and garlic, cooking them for 3 minutes, until the onion is translucent and fragrant. Add the nuts and pumpkin seeds to the vegetables and cook for 2–3 minutes, stirring frequently. If the ingredients begin to stick, add the remaining lard to the pan. Add the seeds (including one tablespoon of the reserved pepper seeds, or more if you like it spicy), the cinnamon stick, and peppercorns and cook for 1 minute, stirring constantly. Add the tortillas and bolillos, stirring to incorporate well. Finally, add the remaining ingredients, including the peppers, to the skillet and simmer on low heat for 15–30 minutes, stirring frequently. Remove the pan from heat and let it stand for 10 minutes.

6. In a blender, puree the mole mixture until smooth. If your food processor doesn't break up the many fine seeds, try running the mixture through the blender in batches. Smother the chicken in mole and enjoy immediately.

Bhindi Masala (Curried Okra)

Okra is a staple crop in the South. Summer heat conditions mean little other than black-eyed peas will set fruit. While fried okra will always be a favorite for this Texas gal, this recipe gives it a run for its money. Feel free to omit the spices for a tamer take on stewed okra if North Indian flavors are not your thing.

Servings: 8 • **Prep time:** 5 mins. • **Cook time:** 15 mins.

Ingredients

- 2 pounds fresh okra
- 1 teaspoon salt, plus more for drying okra
- 2 tablespoons oil
- 1 onion, chopped
- 1½ teaspoons cumin seeds
- ½ teaspoon coriander seeds
- 2 cloves garlic, minced
- 1 cup tomatoes, chopped
- 1 serrano pepper, chopped
- ½ teaspoon ground turmeric
- ½ teaspoon garam masala
- ¼ teaspoon chili powder

1. Wash the okra in cool water and dry with a clean tea towel. Lay the okra on a paper towel and sprinkle it with salt. Let it dry for 10 minutes, then pat it with a paper towel to remove excess moisture. Remove the stems and chop the okra into ½-inch slices.

2. Add the oil to a large cast-iron pot over medium heat. Once the oil is hot, add the onion, cumin seeds, and coriander seeds. Sauté for 3 minutes, stirring frequently. Add the garlic, tomatoes, and remaining ingredients and cook for 1–2 minutes.

3. Add the okra, cover the pot with a lid, and reduce the heat to medium-low. Simmer for about 10 minutes, or until the okra is tender. Stir frequently to prevent sticking. Serve immediately.

Squash Caviar (Kabachkovaya Ikra)

This spread can be made with any varieties of squash (winter squash need only be roasted and their flesh scooped out). Kabachkovaya ikra can be found in jars in grocers throughout Russia and Ukraine. Try it warm or cold, smooth or chunky, served on bread or as a dip. Don't be afraid to experiment and make this recipe your own.

Servings: 4 • **Prep time:** 10 mins. • **Cook time:** 4 hrs.

Ingredients

- 3 assorted squash, peeled and chopped
- 1 large carrot, peeled and chopped
- 1 large onion, peeled and chopped
- 1 bell pepper, seeded, with pith removed
- 4 cloves garlic, peeled and chopped
- 2 tablespoons olive oil
- 2 tablespoons tomato paste
- 1 teaspoon smoked paprika
- ¾ teaspoon salt
- ½ teaspoon black pepper

1. Place all the ingredients in a slow cooker and stir to combine. Heat on low for 4 hours, until the vegetables are tender.
2. Let the squash cool for 10 minutes, then transfer the mixture to a large blender or food processor and blend until smooth. Serve with fresh vegetables, or as a vegan option on a charcuterie board.

Tzatziki Potato Salad

Creamy tzatziki, a yogurt-based dip infused with grated cucumber and fresh dill, is the perfect base for a refreshing fall side.

Servings: 6–8 • **Prep time:** 10 mins. • **Cook time:** 10–15 mins.

Ingredients

- ½ cucumber, grated
- 2 pounds potatoes, chopped
- 3 cloves garlic, grated
- 2 tablespoons olive oil
- ½ cup plain Greek yogurt
- 1 teaspoon salt
- 1 bunch dill, chopped
- 5–7 chives, thinly sliced

1. Bring salted water to boil in a large pot over high heat. As the water boils, strain the grated cucumber in cheesecloth or paper towels to remove any excess moisture. Once the water is boiling, add the chopped potatoes to the pot and cook them for 8–12 minutes, until they are tender. Strain the potatoes and transfer them to the refrigerator to chill for at least 10 minutes.
2. While the potatoes chill, combine the cucumber, garlic, olive, yogurt, salt, and dill in a medium bowl. Stir the cucumber mixture into the chilled potatoes and top with the chives. Store the potato salad in the refrigerator and serve cold.

Irish Boxty Variations

These potato pancakes hailing from Ireland are the perfect vehicle to make use of leftover mashed potatoes. Boxty are fluffy pillows of potato infused with buttery goodness. I've included three topping ideas to get you going.

Servings: 4 • **Prep time:** 5 mins. • **Cook time:** 32 mins.

Ingredients

- 1 cup grated potato (about 2 medium potatoes)
- 1 cup mashed potato
- 1 cup all-purpose flour
- 1 teaspoon baking powder
- 1 teaspoon baking soda
- 2 teaspoons salt
- 2 eggs, beaten
- ¾ cup cream
- ¼ cup butter

1. Strain the potatoes in a fine-mesh sieve. Wring out any excess moisture using a paper towel.
2. In a large bowl, combine all the dry ingredients and the eggs. Add the cream, a little at a time, until a thick batter is formed.
3. Heat the butter over medium-low in a large pan. Once it becomes fragrant, add a ladle of batter. Cook for 4 minutes, or until the bottom has become golden brown. Flip the potato pancake over and cook for 4 minutes.
4. Serve warm with honey, jam, or one of the suggested toppings.

Lamb Boxty with Herbed Apricot Crème Fraîche

Ingredients

- 4 lamb chops (about 1½ to 2 pounds)
- 3 teaspoons salt
- 1½ teaspoons ground pepper
- 3 cloves garlic, minced
- 3 tablespoons fresh rosemary, minced
- ½ cup crème fraîche (or sour cream)
- 2 teaspoons apricot marmalade
- ¼ cup fresh mint
- ¼ teaspoon red pepper flakes

1. Season the lamb chop with sea salt, freshly ground black pepper, minced garlic, and fresh rosemary. Sauté on high for approximately 3 minutes on each side. Let the meat rest for 5 minutes.
2. Pulse the crème fraîche, marmalade, mint, and red pepper flakes until well combined.
3. Slice the lamb thinly and serve over boxty generously drizzled with herbed apricot crème fraîche.

Smoked Salmon Boxty with Dill and Capers

Ingredients

- 2 tablespoons crème fraîche (or sour cream)
- 3 tablespoons fresh dill, chopped, plus more for garnish
- Zest and juice of ½ lemon
- 8 slices smoked salmon (2 slices per boxty)
- 2 tablespoons capers

1. Combine the crème fraîche with the dill and lemon zest and juice in a small bowl.
2. Top the boxty with a generous amount of smoked salmon, a dollop of the dill sauce, capers, and fresh dill.

Boxty with Poached Egg and Mock Hollandaise

Ingredients

- 4 eggs (1 for each boxty)
- ½ cup crème fraîche
- ½ teaspoons English mustard
- Zest and juice of ½ lemon
- 2 teaspoons butter, melted
- Salt, to taste
- Serve with microgreens and green onions

1. Poach an egg for 2–4 minutes, until the egg white is coagulated and the yolk remains mostly runny. In a small bowl, combine the crème fraîche, English mustard, lemon zest and juice, melted butter, and salt until well combined.
2. Spread the mock hollandaise over warm boxty and top with the poached egg, microgreens, and green onion.

Buffalo Cauliflower

Your favorite wings, but vegan! Buffalo cauliflower delivers on flavor and texture when battered in buttermilk and served with (in my humble opinion) the most perfectly balanced sauce. Need I mention the blue cheese dip?

Servings: 4 • **Prep time:** 7 mins. • **Cook time:** 30 mins.

Ingredients
For the cauliflower

- ¾ cup all-purpose flour
- 1 teaspoon salt
- 1 teaspoon garlic powder
- ½ teaspoon paprika
- ¼ teaspoon black pepper
- ¾ cup buttermilk
- 1 head cauliflower, broken into florets

For the buffalo sauce

- ¼ cup cayenne pepper sauce
- ¼ cup sriracha
- 4 tablespoons butter, melted
- 1 tablespoon honey
- 1 teaspoon paprika
- ½ teaspoon garlic powder
- ½ teaspoon chipotle chili powder

For the blue cheese dip

- 2 ounces blue cheese
- ¼ cup Greek yogurt
- ¼ cup mayonnaise
- 1 tablespoon white vinegar
- ¼ teaspoon salt
- ¼ teaspoon sugar
- ⅛ teaspoon black pepper

1. Preheat the oven to 450°F. Line a baking sheet with parchment paper and spray it with cooking spray.
2. Combine the flour, spices, and buttermilk in a rimmed platter. Coat the cauliflower florets with the batter and arrange them in a single layer on the prepared baking sheet. Bake for 30 minutes, until the florets are golden brown.
3. While the cauliflower cooks, prepare the buffalo sauce and blue cheese dip. Whisk together all the ingredients for the buffalo sauce in a medium bowl until smooth. In a separate small bowl, combine the ingredients for the blue cheese dressing until well mixed. Brush the cooked cauliflower with the buffalo sauce and serve with a side of blue cheese dip.

Mushroom and Chèvre Crepes

The creperies of Paris prepare perfect crepes in seconds, usually right before your eyes. Most of us lack the perfect flipping technique or trowel to make a flawless crepe, so I recommend spreading the batter out quickly with a large spatula.

Makes: 10 crepes • **Prep time:** 10 mins. • **Cook time:** 20 mins.

Ingredients

- 1 cup flour
- 2 eggs
- ½ cup whole milk
- ½ cup water
- 3 tablespoons butter, melted, plus 2 tablespoons, plus more as needed
- ¼ teaspoon fine salt, plus more to taste
- 2 tablespoons fresh chives
- 2 tablespoons fresh parsley
- 2 tablespoons fresh mint
- 2 tablespoons fresh dill
- 4 ounces chèvre
- 8 ounces sliced mushrooms
- ½ teaspoons freshly cracked black pepper
- 2 cups arugula

1. In a large bowl, whisk the flour, eggs, milk, water, butter, and salt together until a thin batter is formed. Set it aside to rest.
2. In a separate bowl, fold the fresh herbs and pepper into the chèvre. In a medium pan, melt 2 tablespoons of butter over medium heat. Add the mushrooms, salt, and pepper, and simmer until the mushrooms have cooked down, about 5 minutes. Set aside.
3. Heat a small pad of butter in a nonstick 12-inch skillet over medium heat. Ladle ⅓ cup of the batter into the pan and swirl the pan around until it is evenly covered with a thin layer of batter. Cook the crepe for about 1 minute, until the outer edges have dried out. (Purists will now want to jiggle the pan to ensure the crepe is loose.) Using a circular motion away from your body, flip the crepe over. Novice crepe makers may find it easiest to loosen the crepe edges with a spatula, then, supporting one side with the spatula and the other side with your free hand, invert the crepe. The second side requires only 15–30 seconds to set and cook through to a light golden brown. Cook the remainder of the batter using the same method.
4. To assemble the crepes, spread 2 tablespoons chèvre/herb mixture on each crepe, place ¼ cup of arugula down the center, and spoon the sautéed mushrooms on top.

Nasturtium Salad with Dill Dressing

Nasturtiums are a lovely flower that doubles as a pest trap and pollinator favorite. Their delicate petals and leaves have a peppery finish that can be enjoyed raw or lightly sautéed. Nasturtiums are a beautiful garnish to egg and pasta dishes.

Makes: 4 side salads • **Prep time:** 10 mins.

Ingredients

- 4 cups mixed greens (arugula, kale, beet greens, leaf lettuce, chard)
- 20 nasturtium blooms and leaves
- ½ cup olive oil
- 2 tablespoons lemon juice
- 2 tablespoons Dijon mustard
- ¼ cup fresh dill
- 1 tablespoon maple syrup
- 2 cloves garlic
- 1 teaspoon salt
- ½ teaspoon black pepper

1. Place the greens in a large serving bowl, or on four salad plates. Distribute the nasturtium flowers evenly.
2. Process the remaining ingredients in a food processor or blender, for 30–60 seconds, until the garlic and dill have been finely minced. Dress the salads and season with additional salt and pepper, to taste.

Beef Stir-Fry

Stir-fry is a great way to feature the garden's bounty for any season. Try a summer stir-fry with corn, zucchini, yellow squash, and green beans. Omit the beef or skip the velveting technique to save time and money.

Servings: 4 • **Inactive prep time:** 30 mins. • **Prep time:** 5 mins. • **Cook time:** 20 mins.

Ingredients

- 2 pounds cubed steak/ stew meat
- 1 teaspoon baking soda
- 1 tablespoon sesame oil
- 4 cloves garlic, minced
- 1-inch piece fresh ginger, grated
- 2 large carrots, sliced
- 1 bell pepper, cut into strips
- ½ pound sugar snow peas
- 1 small head broccoli, cut into bite-size stalks
- ¼ cup soy sauce
- 2 tablespoons mirin
- 2 tablespoons honey
- Serve with brown rice or lo mein

1. To tenderize the meat, stir the baking soda into ⅓ cup water until mostly dissolved. Massage the mixture into the meat and let it tenderize for 30 minutes in the refrigerator.
2. Heat the oil in a wok or large sauté pan over high heat. Once the oil becomes fragrant, add the beef and stir-fry for 3 minutes.
3. Add the garlic, ginger, carrots, and bell pepper, cooking for 2 minutes, stirring frequently. Add the remaining ingredients and simmer for 2 minutes, or until crisp and tender. Serve with brown rice or lo mein.

Moroccan Beef Stew

Feature the season's best root vegetables in this kicked-up version of beef stew. The classic Moroccan blend of over a dozen spices, *ras el hanout*, adds a cornucopia of flavor. (Can't find *ras el hanout* in your grocery store? No problem. I included a recipe for that, too.)

Servings: 6 • **Prep time:** 5 mins. • **Cook Time:** 2 hrs. 10 mins.

Ingredients

- 2 tablespoons olive oil
- 2 tablespoons butter
- 3–4 pounds top sirloin roast, lamb roast or boneless leg, or goat rolled loin
- 2 pounds potatoes, chopped
- 2 pounds carrots, chopped
- 1 sweet onion, chopped
- 3 tablespoons *ras el hanout*
- 1 teaspoon salt
- ½ teaspoon black pepper
- 4 cloves garlic, minced
- 1 (14.5 oz) can diced tomatoes
- 1 (15.5 oz) can chickpeas
- 24 ounces beef bone broth

1. In a large pot, heat the oil and butter over medium heat. Add the roast, vegetables, *ras el hanout*, salt, and pepper, cooking for about 7 minutes, stirring frequently.
2. Add the remaining ingredients, along with 15 ounces of water, and cook on medium until boiling. Reduce the heat to low, cover the pot, and simmer for 1½–2 hours, until the meat and vegetables are very tender.

Ras el Hanout

Makes: about ¼ cup
Ingredients

- 2 teaspoons ginger
- 1 teaspoon cumin
- 1 teaspoon coriander
- 1 teaspoon turmeric
- 1 teaspoon salt
- 1 teaspoon cinnamon
- 1 teaspoon paprika
- ¾ teaspoon cardamom
- ¾ teaspoon black pepper
- ½ teaspoon white pepper
- ½ teaspoon cayenne pepper
- ¼ teaspoon cloves
- ¼ teaspoon allspice

1. Combine all the ground spices well. If using seeds or pods, first roast them in a dry skillet for 3 minutes, stirring frequently.
2. Once the spices are slightly cooled, grind them in a clean coffee grinder. Store in an airtight container for 3 months.

Lemon Doro Wot with Eggplant

Doro wot (also spelled wat) is a spiced chicken stew originating in Ethiopia. Warm berbere spice marries perfectly with eggplant and tomato. You can find berbere in the spice aisle of most grocery stores or online from a spice vendor.

Servings: 4 • **Prep time:** 25 mins. • **Cook time:** 1 hr.

Ingredients

- 2 tablespoons butter, plus more as needed
- 2 tablespoons olive oil
- 1 large onion, sliced
- 4 cloves garlic, minced
- 6 chicken legs, skin on
- ¼ cup berbere
- ½ eggplant, cut into ½-inch pieces
- 2 cups chicken stock
- 6 ounces tomato paste
- Juice of 1 lemon
- 1 lemon, sliced
- Serve with rice, couscous, or flatbread

1. Preheat the oven to 425°F. Heat the butter and olive oil in a large cast-iron pan over medium heat. Once the butter has melted, add the onion and sauté for 3 minutes, stirring occasionally. Add the garlic and cook for 30 seconds.
2. Place the chicken into the pan, add butter and the berbere spice, stirring to combine the mixture well. Brown the chicken on each side for 6–8 minutes. Finally, add the eggplant, chicken stock, tomato paste, and lemon juice, and stir well.
3. Arrange the lemon slices in between drumsticks and place the chicken in the oven. Bake for 35–40 minutes. Serve with rice, couscous, or flatbread.

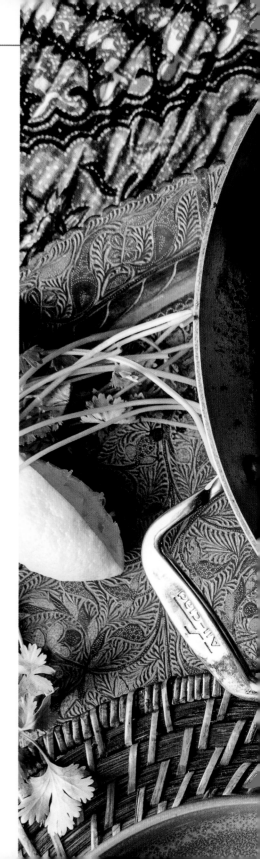

Show-Stopping Apple Pie

Be it Thanksgiving dinner or a church potluck, this pie will be the talk of the table. With a wheat crust and less than half the sugar, this pie is easy on the eyes and the waistline. Don't forget to casually mention that as gawkers swoon at the site of this beauty.

Makes: 1 pie • **Prep time:** 20 mins. • **Inactive prep time:** 40 mins. • **Cook time:** 50 mins.

Ingredients
For the wheat pie crust
- ¾ cup wheat flour
- ½ cup all-purpose flour
- ½ teaspoon salt
- 1 tablespoon sugar
- ¼ teaspoon baking powder
- ¼ cup shortening, cold and cubed
- ¼ cup unsalted butter, cold and cubed
- 2–3 tablespoons cold milk

For the apple filling
- 4 tablespoons unsalted butter
- 4 large apples (I recommend Fuji), rinsed and cored, sliced across the center in thin slices
- 4 tablespoons sugar
- Juice of 1 lemon
- 1 tablespoon apricot jelly, melted

1. To make the crust, mix the dry ingredients in a large bowl. Using your fingers or a pastry blender, quickly work in the butter and shortening until the pieces are pea sized. Add enough milk to get a soft dough formed, taking care not to overmix. Place the dough in the refrigerator for at least 30 minutes.
2. Preheat the oven to 375°F. Remove the pie crust from the refrigerator and let it rest at room temperature for 10 minutes. Roll out the dough and place it in a deep-dish pie pan. Prick the dough all over with a fork. Bake it for 15–20 minutes, until the pastry begins to turn golden around the edges.
3. To make the filling, melt the butter in a large sauté pan over low-medium heat. Add the apple slices then sprinkle them with the sugar and lemon juice. Cover the apples and stir occasionally, until they become malleable, about 5 minutes. Remove them from the pan and place them on a clean workspace, reserving the cooking liquid.
4. Place three layers of apples at the bottom of the prepared pie crust. Cut a slit across the radius of the remaining apple slices. Fold an apple slice in on itself until a spiral shape is formed. Keep adding more apple slices until you've reached the desired size of your rose. Repeat until your pie has been filled. Pour the reserved apple cooking liquid over the finished roses. Brush the apples and crust with the apricot preserves. If desired, return the pie to the oven for 20 minutes, or until it is heated through.

Cinnamon-Swirl Apple Cake

Meet your newest go-to dessert for apple season. This cake is easy, fail-proof, and fills the house with the best fragrances of fall.

Servings: 8 • **Prep time:** 15 mins. • **Cook time:** 1 hr.

Ingredients
For the cake batter
- 1½ cups brown sugar
- ⅓ cup vegetable oil
- 1 cup Greek yogurt
- 1 egg
- 1 tablespoon dark rum
- 1 teaspoon vanilla
- 2 apples, chopped, plus 1 apple, grated
- 2½ cups all-purpose flour
- 1 teaspoon baking soda

For the cinnamon swirl
- 3 tablespoons melted butter
- 2 tablespoons brown sugar
- 1 tablespoon cinnamon

1. Preheat the oven to 325°F. To make the batter, in a large bowl or stand mixer, combine all the ingredients and mix until just combined. Transfer it to a greased 9 x 13-inch pan.
2. To make the cinnamon swirl, in a separate small bowl, combine all the ingredients. Spoon the cinnamon swirl on top of the batter and use a knife or spatula to make big swirls across the pan. Repeat this technique going in the opposite direction to finish dispersing the swirl.
3. Bake for 50–60 minutes, until the cake is set and a toothpick inserted into the center of the cake comes out clean.

Citrus Basil Harissa Shrimp

Harissa has become a staple seasoning in our home. Its smoky flavor profile is endlessly versatile, perfect on vegetable and meat dishes alike. Though harissa is widely available at most grocers (try the international aisle), homemade harissa is an ingenious way to use up the last of the season's peppers.

Servings: 2 main courses or 4 appetizer portions • **Prep time:** 5 mins. • **Cook time:** 6–10 mins.

Ingredients

- 1 pound gulf jumbo shrimp, tails on
- 1 tablespoon harissa (see recipe below)
- 1 tablespoon vegetable oil
- Juice of 1 orange
- ¼ cup packed fresh basil, chopped
- 1 teaspoon salt
- Serve with couscous or rice

1. Combine all the ingredients in a large bowl and mix them well. On a grill preheated to medium, cook the shrimp for 2–3 minutes on each side, until the shrimp become opaque and begin to curl.
2. Remove the shrimp from the grill and serve with couscous or rice.

Harissa

Makes: about ¾ cup

Ingredients

- 4 ounces dried hot chiles (combination of ancho, guajillo, and pasilla)
- 2 teaspoons coriander seeds
- 1½ teaspoons cumin seeds
- 1 teaspoon caraway seeds
- 3 cloves garlic
- ½ teaspoon salt
- ¼ cup olive oil
- Juice of 1 lemon

1. In a dry skillet over medium heat, roast the peppers and seeds for about 5 minutes, stirring frequently.
2. Remove the skillet from heat and seed and stem all the peppers. Transfer the peppers and spice mixture to a food processor and add the remaining ingredients. Blend until a smooth paste forms. Serve immediately.

Kale Salad with Roasted Chicken, Goat Cheese, Pepitas, and Crumbled Bacon

Recipe inspiration comes from all kinds of places. In the case of this kale salad, I put all my favorite ingredients together into a colorful, crisp taste of autumn.

Servings: 2 entree portions • **Prep time:** 25 mins. • **Inactive time:** 10–15 mins.

Ingredients
For the salad

- 2 tablespoons rice wine vinegar
- 1 tablespoon sugar
- 1 teaspoon salt
- 3 radishes, chopped
- 4 cups kale, chopped, with stems removed
- 1 leg quarter rotisserie chicken, shredded
- 1 crisp apple, chopped
- 3 tablespoons pumpkin seeds, roasted and salted
- 2 tablespoons bacon, crumbled
- 1 ounce goat cheese, crumbled
- 3 green onions, chopped

For the vinaigrette

- ¾ cup olive oil
- ⅓ cup vinegar (I recommend sherry, champagne, or white wine vinegar)
- 1 tablespoon Dijon mustard, plus 1 teaspoon
- 2 tablespoons maple syrup
- 2 cloves garlic, grated
- 1 teaspoon salt
- ½ teaspoon cayenne

1. To begin making the salad, in a medium bowl, combine 2 tablespoons of water with the rice wine vinegar. Stir in the sugar and salt until they have dissolved. Add the radishes and let them pickle for 10–15 minutes.
2. Combine the salad ingredients in a large serving bowl. To make the vinaigrette, in a separate bowl, whisk together all the ingredients until well combined. Drizzle the vinaigrette over the salad before serving.

Kale Salad with Roasted Chicken, Goat Cheese, Pepitas, and Crumbled Bacon • **153**

Roasted Pumpkin

Cutting open a pumpkin can be a bit of a chore. An easy (and arguably fun) way to split a pumpkin open is to drop it from a small elevation. Most pumpkins will happily break into two or three manageable pieces when they are dropped from shoulder height onto a sidewalk or porch.

Prep time: 10 mins. • **Cook time:** 35–45 mins.

Ingredients
- ❦ 1 pumpkin or large squash (3–20 pounds)

1. Preheat the oven to 375°F. Cut the pumpkin or squash in half and scrape out the seeds and pith. Reserve the seeds for roasting later. If the pumpkin is larger than 5 pounds, cut it into smaller pieces to reduce the cooking time.
2. Place the pumpkin flesh side down on a baking sheet and add 1 cup of water to the bottom of the pan, then place it in the oven. After 20 minutes, check and add more water if necessary. Cook the pumpkin until it is fork tender.

Pumpkin Risotto

Simple and satisfying, make this risotto on a cold fall day with the season's remaining pumpkins.

Servings: 4 • **Prep time:** 15 mins. • **Cook time:** 30 mins.

Ingredients

- 4–5 cups chicken or vegetable stock
- 2 tablespoons olive oil
- 2 shallots, chopped
- 2 cloves garlic, minced
- 1½ cups arborio rice
- ½ cup dry white wine (I recommend vermouth or pino grigio)
- 1 teaspoon salt
- ½ teaspoon freshly ground black pepper
- ½ teaspoon poultry seasoning
- ¼ teaspoon nutmeg (or 4 grates of a fresh nutmeg)
- 1 pound roasted pumpkin, diced
- 1 cup grated Pecorino cheese

1. In a medium saucepan, heat the stock until it begins to simmer. Reduce the heat so that the stock remains hot.
2. In a large cast-iron or heavy-bottomed pan, heat the olive oil over medium heat. Sauté the shallots for 2 minutes. Add the garlic and rice, stirring frequently, and sauté until the rice begins to release a nutty flavor. Add the wine to the pan, stirring to incorporate the ingredients until the liquid has been mostly absorbed, about 5 minutes.
3. Ladle in ½ cup of the warm stock, stirring with a non-reactive spoon until the liquid has been absorbed. Add another ½ cup of stock and repeat, letting it become absorbed, until the rice becomes creamy but still has a small amount of bite to it. Remove the pan from heat and stir in the remaining ingredients. Serve ⅓ cup for a side portion or ⅔ cup for a meal portion.

Colonial Pumpkin Pie

A formidable history expert, my husband often brings me vintage recipes from different eras. This pumpkin "pie" closely resembles a crustless recipe from colonial America circa 1600.

Servings: 8–10 • **Prep time:** 15 mins. • **Cook time:** 3 hrs. 5 mins.

Ingredients
For the pie

- 1 teaspoon cinnamon
- ½ teaspoon nutmeg
- ½ cup brown sugar, packed
- 10–12 pounds pumpkin, top, seeds, and pulp removed
- 2 apples, diced (I recommend pink lady, granny smith, or Fuji)
- 1 cup raisins
- 1 cup chopped pecans
- 8 tablespoons butter, cubed

For vanilla bean sauce

- 2 cups heavy cream
- ½ cup granulated sugar
- Pinch of salt
- 2 tablespoons rum or brandy (optional)
- 4 tablespoons butter
- 1 vanilla bean

1. Preheat the oven to 350°F. To begin making the pie, combine the spices and brown sugar in a small bowl.
2. Place the pumpkin on a rimmed, aluminum foil–lined cookie sheet. Place half of the apples in the bottom of the pumpkin and top the apples with ½ cup raisins, ½ cup pecans, and half of the butter. Top the fruit and nut mixture with half of the sugar-spice mixture. Using the remaining pie ingredients, repeat the process to form a second layer inside the pumpkin.
3. Cover pumpkin with aluminum foil and transfer it to the oven. Bake for 3 hours, or until the pumpkin flesh is fork tender and the filling is bubbling.
4. To make the vanilla bean sauce, in a medium saucepan, combine cream, sugar, salt, liquor (optional), and butter over medium-low heat. Using a paring knife, cut down the length of the vanilla bean and scrape its contents into the cream mixture. Whisk the sauce until it is bubbling, and a creamy consistency is reached. Serve it warm by spooning the sauce over each serving of pumpkin pie.

Pumpkin Cinnamon Rolls

Homemade cinnamon rolls are a labor of love and completely worth every minute. My daughters and I like to make these in our PJ's on chilly Saturday mornings.

Makes: 1 dozen rolls • **Prep time:** 20 mins. • **Inactive prep time:** 1½ hrs. • **Cook time:** 25 mins.

Ingredients
For the dough

- 1 cup whole milk
- 6 tablespoons butter
- ⅓ cup sugar
- 2¼ teaspoons (1 packet) instant yeast
- 1 cup roasted pumpkin, pureed
- 3½ cups all-purpose flour
- 1 teaspoon pumpkin spice
- ½ teaspoon cinnamon
- ¼ teaspoon salt

For the filling

- 1 cup brown sugar
- ⅓ cup roasted pumpkin, pureed
- 2 tablespoons butter, melted
- 2 teaspoons cinnamon

For the frosting

- 4 ounces cream cheese, at room temperature
- 1 cup confectioner's sugar
- 2 tablespoons whole milk
- 1 teaspoon vanilla extract
- Pinch of salt

1. To begin making the dough, combine the milk, butter, and sugar in a large saucepan over medium heat, stirring frequently, until the mixture is warm to the touch, about 120°F. Add the yeast and stir to combine. Let it stand for 5 minutes, until it is foamy. Stir in the pumpkin.

2. In a separate bowl, combine the dry ingredients. Stir them into the pumpkin-yeast mixture until well combined. Knead the dough by hand or in a stand mixer for about 7 minutes, until a smooth, elastic dough is formed. Let it sit in a warm place for at least 1 hour, or until it has doubled in size.

3. To make the filling, in a medium-sized bowl, combine all the ingredients. Once the dough has doubled in size, tip it onto a floured

work surface. Roll the dough out to about a 12 x 15-inch rectangle. Brush on the filling until the entire surface of the dough is covered. Starting with the longer side, roll the dough tightly, in the style of a jelly roll. Using dental floss, cut the roll into 9–12 sections. Place the pieces cut side down into a 9 x 13-inch pan and cover it with a kitchen towel. Let it proof for 30–60 minutes.

4. Remove the towel and bake the roll for 20–25 minutes, or until the center has set. Cool the roll on a wire rack.

5. To make the frosting, combine all the ingredients in a large bowl or stand mixer and beat until smooth. Spread the frosting evenly on cooled buns and enjoy.

Five Variations on Muffins

Muffins can be sweet or savory, but they're always delicious, filling, and the perfect start to a cozy, autumn day.

Makes: 12 muffins • **Prep time:** 5–25 mins. • **Cook time:** 15–20 mins.

Ingredients

- 2 cups sifted flour (all-purpose, whole wheat, or almond)
- 1½ teaspoons baking powder
- 1 teaspoon baking soda
- ½ teaspoon fine salt
- ½ cup granulated sugar
- ¼ cup brown sugar
- 8 tablespoons (1 stick) unsalted butter, softened
- 2 eggs
- 1 teaspoon vanilla extract
- ½ teaspoon almond extract
- ¾ cup yogurt or sour cream
- ¼ cup milk

1. Preheat the oven to 400°F. Oil a standard-size muffin tin with nonstick spray.
2. Whisk the dry ingredients together in a large bowl. In a separate large bowl or the bowl of your stand mixer, beat together the butter and sugars until the mixture is light and creamy. With the mixer running, add in the eggs one at a time, mixing well. Mix in the extracts.
3. Pour the dry ingredients into the wet ingredients and mix for 3–5 seconds. Scrape down the side of the bowl before adding the milk and yogurt, then mix until just combined.
4. Spoon the batter to fill the top of each muffin cup (I find a ⅓-cup measuring cup or a ladle works well for this). Place the muffin tin on the center rack and bake for 15–20 minutes, until a toothpick inserted into one of the centrally located muffins comes out clean. Cool the muffins on a cooling rack for 3–5 minutes before enjoying.

Morning Glory Muffins
Ingredients

- 1 teaspoon cinnamon
- ½ teaspoon ginger
- ¼ teaspoon nutmeg
- ¼ cup orange juice
- 2 cups shredded carrots
- ½ cup raisins
- ½ cup walnuts

1. Whisk the cinnamon, ginger, and nutmeg into the dry ingredients of the master recipe. Substitute the milk in the master recipe for orange juice.
2. Once the dry and wet ingredients have been combined in step 3 of the master recipe, fold in the carrots, raisins, and walnuts before baking. Proceed with the master recipe as written.

Zucchini Muffins
Ingredients

- 1½ teaspoons ground cinnamon
- 2 cups zucchini, grated
- 1 cup walnuts

1. Whisk the ground cinnamon into the dry ingredients as in step 2 of the master recipe. Once the wet and dry ingredients have been combined in step 3 of the master recipe, fold in the zucchini and walnuts. Proceed with the master recipe as written.

Carrot Cake Muffins

Ingredients

For the muffins

- 1¼ teaspoons ground cinnamon
- ¾ teaspoon ground ginger
- ¼ teaspoon nutmeg
- ⅛ teaspoon cloves
- 2 cups grated carrots
- 1 cup toasted pecans
- ½ cup golden raisins

For the frosting (optional)

- 16 ounces cream cheese
- 3 cups confectioner's sugar
- 1 teaspoon vanilla extract
- Pinch of salt

1. Whisk the cinnamon, ginger, nutmeg, and cloves into the dry ingredients as in step 2 of the master recipe. Once the wet and dry ingredients have been combined in step 3 of the master recipe, fold in the carrots, pecans, and golden raisins.
2. Proceed with the master recipe as written. If you like, you can easily transition these muffins to cupcakes by topping them with the whipped frosting mixture, waiting until the muffins have cooled before frosting them.

Triple Berry Muffins

Ingredients

- ½ cup blueberries
- ½ cup strawberries, tops removed and chopped
- ½ cup raspberries

1. Once the wet and dry ingredients have been combined in step 3 of the master recipe, fold in the blueberries, strawberries, and raspberries. Proceed with the recipe as written.

Pumpkin Muffins

Ingredients

For the muffins

- 1½ teaspoons ground cinnamon
- ½ teaspoon ground nutmeg
- ¼ teaspoon ground ginger
- 1 cup pumpkin flesh, baked

For the streusel topping

- 1 cup all-purpose flour
- ½ cup brown sugar
- 1 teaspoon cinnamon
- 1 (4 oz) stick of butter

1. Whisk the cinnamon, nutmeg, and ginger into the dry ingredients as in step 2 of the master recipe.
2. Add the pumpkin to the wet ingredients in step 2 of the master recipe before mixing them with the dry ingredients. To make the cinnamon streusel topping, mix the dry ingredients together then cut in the butter. Top the muffin batter with the streusel prior to baking as instructed in step 4 of the master recipe.

Winter

I wait all year for the salads of winter. It's a counterintuitive thing—most of us think of salads as a dish for summer. But butter crunch, romaine, kale, and chard sweeten and crisp with cooler weather. The first hard frost will kill most tender greens, but heartier collards, cabbages, broccoli, and mustards hang on, thrive even.

My family and I make the most of what's left of winter's greens before they bolt. We snip turnip greens all winter and into spring until they're bug-eaten, then harvest the turnips that stay content and well insulated in the ground.

I take great pleasure from mashing the season's first potato and spinning a generous handful of arugula. Greens are added to every soup and stirred into eggs most mornings. I stuff, sauté, roast, and bake winter squash for everyday use. Carrots sweeten frittatas and snuggle with pork roasts in the slow cooker. Life seems to have a slower pace, which I relish before the transformation of spring.

Winter is a time to savor a slower pace, enjoying sweet, warming meals made with the heartier vegetables that flourish despite the frost.

In Season

Acorn squash

Brussels sprouts

Butternut squash

Cabbage

Carrots

Celery

Cilantro

Collard greens

Delicata squash

Dill

Fennel

Grapefruit

Kale

Lettuce

Mustard greens

Oranges

Pears

Persimmons

Pomegranates

Potatoes

Pumpkins

Rutabagas

Thyme

Turnips

Yams

Squash Gratin

This dish is pure comfort: creamy, aromatic, and flavorful with a gorgeous cheesy crust on top!

Makes: one 9 x 13-inch pan • **Prep time:** 5 mins. • **Cook time:** 40 mins.

Ingredients

- 6 tablespoons butter, plus 2 tablespoons
- 8 cloves garlic, minced
- 2 pounds winter squash (butternut, delicata, acorn), peeled and chopped
- Salt and pepper, to taste
- 1 cup heavy cream
- 1 teaspoon thyme
- ½ teaspoon poultry seasoning
- 1 cup grated gruyere, divided
- 8 slices sourdough or crusty white bread, cubed

1. Preheat the oven to 400°F. Heat the butter over medium heat in a large sauté pan. Once the butter is melted and aromatic, add the garlic and cook for 30 seconds, stirring frequently. Add the squash to the pan, season it with salt and pepper, and cook for 8 minutes, stirring to prevent sticking.
2. Remove the pan from heat and add in the heavy cream, thyme, poultry seasoning, ½ cup of gruyere, and half of the cubed bread. Scrape the bottom of the pan.
3. Grease a 9 x 13-inch baking dish with butter. Transfer the squash mixture to the prepared dish and top it with remaining bread and gruyere. Bake for 30 minutes, until the cheese is bubbly and the bread has turned golden brown.

Butternut Bisque

This decadent bisque makes a wonderful party hors d'oeuvre when served in a festive glass.

Servings: 4–6 • **Prep time:** 10 mins. • **Cook time:** 40 mins.

Ingredients

- 2 tablespoons unsalted butter
- 1 large sweet onion, diced
- 2 cloves garlic, minced
- 3 pounds butternut squash, peeled and cubed
- 4 cups chicken stock
- 1 tablespoon brown sugar
- 2 teaspoons salt
- ¼ teaspoon poultry seasoning
- ⅛ teaspoon ground ginger
- 2 bay leaves
- Pinch of nutmeg
- ¾ cup whipping cream

1. In a large pot, heat the butter over medium heat. Add the onion and sauté for 2–3 minutes, stirring frequently, until the onion is fragrant and beginning to turn translucent. Add the garlic and sauté for 1 minute, stirring frequently. Add all the remaining ingredients except for the cream. Bring the soup to a vigorous boil and reduce the heat to medium-low.
2. Cook for 25–35 minutes, stirring occasionally, until the squash is fork tender. Remove the bay leaves, then remove the soup from the heat and add the cream.
3. Allow the soup to cool slightly, then puree it with an immersion blender or in a food processor until well blended. Serve it in cocktail or shot glasses.

Butternut Squash Pie with Pecan Streusel

Thanks to its higher sugar content and robust flavor, homegrown butternut squash makes a pie that rivals any pumpkin or sweet potato. A crunchy pecan streusel takes this treat to the next level.

Servings: 8–10 • **Prep time:** 20 mins. • **Cook time:** 55–60 mins.

Ingredients

For the pie crust

- 1¼ cups all-purpose flour, plus extra for dusting
- 1 stick unsalted butter, cold, diced
- ⅛ teaspoon salt
- 1 tablespoon sugar, plus 1 teaspoon
- ¼ cup cold water

For the filling

- 3 pounds butternut squash, roasted, skins removed
- 1¼ cups whipping cream
- 2 eggs
- ⅔ cup brown sugar, packed
- 1 teaspoon cinnamon
- ½ teaspoon ground nutmeg
- ¼ teaspoon ground ginger
- ¼ teaspoon ground cloves
- ¼ teaspoon fine salt

For the pecan streusel

- ¾ cup chopped pecans, roasted
- 2 tablespoons brown sugar
- ¼ cup all-purpose flour
- ¼ teaspoon cinnamon
- 2 tablespoons unsalted butter, cold, diced

1. Preheat the oven to 425°F. To make the pie crust, in a food processor, combine the flour, butter, salt, and sugar and pulse until chickpea-size bits are formed. Slowly add the water and stop pulsing as soon as the ingredients begin to come together. Form the dough into a ball, cover it with oiled cling wrap, and place it in the refrigerator while you prepare the filling.
2. To make the filling, combine all the ingredients in a food processor and pulse until smooth, about 2 minutes. Scrape the side of the bowl and set the filling aside.
3. Remove the dough from the refrigerator. Sprinkle a prep surface and rolling pin with a generous amount of flour. Roll out the dough until it forms an 11-inch round. Transfer it to a 9-inch pie pan and fold the extra dough under around the edges. Use your fingers to crimp the edges of the pie shell, or use a fork to make indentions along the crust. Pour the filling into the shell.
4. Bake for 15 minutes. Meanwhile, combine all the ingredients for the pecan streusel using your hands or a pastry blender, until the streusel is crumbly and the butter is well incorporated. Decrease the oven temperature to 350°F and cook the pie for 30 minutes, until the filling is almost firm. Add the streusel topping and cook for 10–15 minutes, or until the topping is golden brown and the middle of the pie is set.

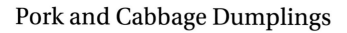

Pork and Cabbage Dumplings

Chinese five spice is a blend of Sichuan pepper, cinnamon, cloves, star anise, and fennel that is available at most grocers. Lining your steamer basket with fresh cabbage leaves keeps the dumplings from sticking to the bottom and sides.

Makes: 40 dumplings • **Prep time:** 15 mins. • **Cook time:** 25 mins.

Ingredients
For the dumplings

- 1 pound ground pork
- 3 cups cabbage, shredded
- 2 green onions, thinly sliced
- 2 cloves garlic, minced
- 2 tablespoons soy sauce
- 1 egg
- 1 teaspoon fresh ginger, grated
- 1 teaspoon Chinese five spice (optional)
- ¼ teaspoon salt
- ¼ Sichuan pepper
- 1 package wonton wrappers

For the dipping sauce

- ¼ cup soy sauce
- 2 tablespoons rice wine vinegar
- 1 clove garlic, grated
- 1 tablespoon honey
- 1 tablespoon toasted sesame oil

1. Combine the ground pork, cabbage, green onion, garlic, soy sauce, egg, ginger, Chinese five spice (if using), salt, and pepper in a large bowl. Mix until well combined.
2. Place a spoonful of the filling on the center of a wonton wrapper and seal using the method you are most comfortable with. You can use a little water on your fingers to help seal the dumplings. Repeat with the remaining filling and wonton wrappers, or prepare as many as desired.
3. Place a double boiler with at least 2 inches of water in the bottom over high heat. Line a steamer basket with cabbage leaves and arrange the uncooked wontons inside, leaving about ½ inch of space between them. Steam the wontons for 7–10 minutes, or until a toothpick inserted into the center of a wonton comes out clean. Repeat for the remaining batches of wontons.
4. To make the dipping sauce, in a small bowl, whisk together all the ingredients until the honey is dissolved. Serve the wontons immediately with the dipping sauce.

South African Gem Squash Stuffed with Moroccan Beef

This recipe lends itself to substitutions, so please feel free to play around with the variety of winter squash or ancient grain. Ground lamb would be a lovely stand-in for ground beef.

Servings: 4 • **Cooking time:** 1 hr. • **Prep time:** 20 mins.

Ingredients

- 1 winter squash, halved, seeds and pith removed
- Salt, to taste
- 1 tablespoon butter
- 1 cup chicken broth
- ½ cup red quinoa
- 1 cup walnuts, chopped
- 1 tablespoon olive oil
- ½ medium onion, chopped
- 1 pound ground beef
- 3 cloves garlic, minced
- 3 dates, pitted and chopped
- 2 teaspoons cinnamon
- ½ teaspoon cumin
- ½ teaspoon ground ginger (or 1 generous teaspoon fresh ginger, grated)
- Red pepper flakes, to taste
- 1 large bunch fresh spearmint

1. Preheat the oven to 400°F. Place the squash flesh side up on a baking dish and sprinkle it with salt. Divide the butter in half and place one-half inside each squash cavity. Add about 1 inch of water to the bottom of the baking dish and bake the squash for approximately 45 minutes to 1 hour, or until it is fork tender.
2. About 20 minutes into roasting the squash, place the chicken broth and quinoa in a small saucepan over medium heat. Bring it to a boil, cover the pan, and reduce the heat to low. Cook for 10–15 minutes, stirring occasionally. Strain to remove any excess broth, as needed.
3. Place the walnuts in a large sauté pan over medium heat. Stirring frequently to prevent burning, cook for 3–5 minutes, until the walnuts are fragrant. Remove them from the pan and set them aside.
4. Add the oil and onion to the pan, cooking for 2 minutes until the onion begins to turn translucent. Add the remaining ingredients to the onion mixture and cook for 7–10 minutes, until the ground beef is cooked through. Add the prepared quinoa and walnuts.
5. Fill each squash cavity with the quinoa-beef mixture and enjoy.

Turnip Green Dip

Turnip greens add a spicier kick to what would be a formidable spinach dip. Ladle this dip on tortilla chips, fresh carrots, or toasted baguettes.

Servings: 6 • **Prep time:** 5 mins. • **Cook time:** 30 mins.

Ingredients

- 1 pound fresh bacon, chopped
- ½ onion, finely chopped
- 2 cloves garlic, minced
- ¼ cup white wine
- 4 heaping cups packed fresh turnip greens, stemmed and chopped
- 1 cup sour cream
- 8 ounces cream cheese
- 4 ounces mayonnaise
- ½ cup Parmigiano Reggiano
- ¼ teaspoon red pepper flakes
- ¼ teaspoon salt
- ¼ cup fresh mozzarella, shredded
- Serve with crudité or toasted baguette

1. In a large sauté pan, cook the bacon until crisp. Transfer the bacon to a plate lined with paper towels.
2. Sauté the onions in the bacon drippings over medium heat for 2 minutes, or until they are almost translucent. Add the garlic and wine and cook for 1–2 minutes. Stir in the turnip greens and the remaining ingredients except for the mozzarella and cook for 6–8 minutes, or until the cream cheese is melted. Stir in the bacon.
3. Transfer the dip to a baking dish and top it with the mozzarella. Broil the dip on high for 4–5 minutes, until the cheese is golden brown. Serve hot with crudité or a toasted baguette.

Hasselback Rutabagas

The rutabaga is the love child of a turnip and a cabbage. The cruciferous genes in rutabagas give them a nutrient boost: they're full of fiber and vitamins C and B6. Homegrown rutabagas are best harvested after a few frosts, when their roots are still small and tender.

Servings: 6–8 • **Prep time:** 15 mins. • **Cook time:** 50 mins.

Ingredients

- 2 rutabagas (3 pounds), scrubbed and cut in half
- ½ cup Garlic Herb Butter (see recipe on page 63), softened
- 1 teaspoon paprika
- ¾ teaspoon salt
- ½ teaspoon black pepper
- ¼ cup cotija cheese
- ¼ cup bacon crumbles
- 2 tablespoons fresh parsley, chopped

1. Preheat the oven to 425°F. Line a baking sheet with aluminum foil and spray the foil with nonstick cooking spray.
2. Wash and scrub rutabagas to remove any soil. Peel and quarter clean rutabagas. With the flat, cut side down on the cutting board, place two chopsticks or wooden spoons on either side of a rutabaga quarter. Starting from the outer edge, make a thin slice (about ⅛ inch thick) in the rutabaga, guiding the knife down until it reaches the chopstick. The chopsticks will prevent you from slicing the rutabaga all the way through, leaving about ¼ inch of the bottom unsliced. Move another ⅛ inch down the rutabaga and make another slice. Continue this process until you have sliced down the entire length of the rutabaga. Repeat for the remaining rutabaga quarters.
3. Transfer the sliced rutabagas to the prepared baking sheet. Slather each rutabaga with the garlic herb butter using a pastry brush or your hands, taking care to get butter in between the slices. Season the rutabagas with paprika, salt, and pepper. Cook for 50 minutes, until the rutabagas are tender and browned.
4. Remove the rutabagas from the oven and let them cool for 5–10 minutes. Top with cheese, bacon, and parsley before serving.

Southern Collard Greens

Tougher greens like collards and cabbage benefit from a longer cooking time to break down their fibrous cells. Simmering on low softens the bitter phenolic compounds in the collards.

Servings: 6 • **Prep Time:** 15 mins. • **Cook time:** 1 hr.

Ingredients

- ½ pound bacon, roughly chopped
- ½ large sweet onion, chopped
- 1½ teaspoons red pepper flakes
- 4 garlic cloves, minced
- 2 bunches (about 6 cups) collard greens, rinsed, stemmed, and roughly chopped
- 2 cups low-sodium low-fat chicken stock, plus 1 cup
- Sea salt, to taste

1. Sauté the bacon, onions, and red pepper flakes in a large pot over medium-high heat, until the onions become translucent and the bacon begins to brown.
2. Add the garlic and stir until fragrant, about 30 seconds. Add the remaining ingredients, cover the pot, and simmer for 45 minutes to 2 hours. Serve warm.

Creamed Greens

The ultimate in comfort food, these creamy greens are a great side for Christmas dinner or New Year's lunch.

Servings: 4–6 • **Prep time:** 10 mins. • **Cook time:** 30 mins.

Ingredients

- ½ pound fresh bacon, chopped
- 3 tablespoons butter
- 2 shallots, chopped
- 4 cloves garlic, minced
- 2 tablespoons all-purpose flour
- 2 cups heavy cream
- 2 cups milk
- Generous splash of apple cider vinegar
- ⅛ teaspoon nutmeg
- 2 pounds mixed young greens (I recommend spinach, kale, swiss chard, beet greens, and/or collards)

1. Place the bacon in a deep sauté pan on medium heat and cook until crisp, about 5 minutes. Remove the bacon from the pan with a slotted spoon and place it on a paper towel–lined plate. Add the butter to the drippings in the pan.
2. Add the shallots and cook for 2 minutes. Add the garlic and cook for 30 seconds. Stir in the flour and cook for 2 minutes, until the flour is golden brown. Add the remaining ingredients (including the reserved bacon) and cook for 20 minutes, stirring frequently, until the sauce has thickened and the greens are wilted.

Spinach and Kale Frittata

Frittatas are the perfect way to incorporate seasonal produce into breakfast, a meal that often misses out on healthy vegetables. And, accompanied by a green salad or bowl of mixed fruits, frittatas are just as good for lunch or dinner.

Servings: 6 • **Prep time:** 10 mins. • **Cook time:** 15 mins.

Ingredients

- ½ pound fresh bacon, roughly chopped
- ½ medium onion, finely chopped
- 2 carrots, chopped
- 3 cloves garlic, minced
- 1 cup spinach, rinsed and roughly chopped
- 1 cup kale, rinsed, stemmed, and roughly chopped
- ½ cup mushrooms, sliced
- Salt and pepper, to taste
- 8 eggs, beaten
- ½ cup fresh dill, chopped
- 1 cup shredded cheese (I recommend mozzarella, gruyere, or cheddar)
- Serve with avocadoes, sliced, and sour cream

1. Set the oven to high broil. Using a 12-inch oven-safe sauté pan, cook the bacon over medium heat until brown. Set aside the bacon on a paper towel–lined plate. Drain off the rendered fat until 2 tablespoons remain in the pan. Add the onion and carrots and cook for 3 minutes, stirring occasionally. Add the garlic, greens, and mushrooms, cooking for 2–3 minutes, until the greens are wilted. Season the mixture with salt and pepper.
2. In a bowl, combine the eggs, dill, and bacon. Pour the egg mixture into the pan and cook on medium-low until the eggs begin to set, 4–5 minutes. Top the frittata with the cheese and place the pan into the oven. Broil for 1–3 minutes, or until the cheese begins to turn golden brown. Enjoy with a slice of fresh avocado and a dollop of sour cream.

Root Vegetables with Agrodolce

Agro ("sour") and *dolce* ("sweet") is an Italian condiment made by reducing vinegar with sugar or honey. Freely substitute balsamic or wine vinegar and maple, agave, or coconut syrup as preferred.

Servings: 4 • **Prep time:** 7 mins. • **Cook time:** 30 mins.

Ingredients

- 2 pounds root vegetables (turnips, radishes, rutabagas, parsnips, carrots, potatoes, yams, etc.), scrubbed, ends removed
- ⅓ cup olive oil
- 3 tablespoons sherry vinegar
- 1 tablespoon honey
- ¾ teaspoon salt
- ½ teaspoon pepper

1. Preheat the oven to 400°F. Chop the vegetables into 1-inch pieces.
2. Combine the remaining ingredients in a large bowl to make the agrodolce. Add the vegetables to the agrodolce and massage the sauce to coat the vegetables. Transfer the vegetables to a baking sheet and roast for 30 minutes, stirring every 10 minutes.

Thai Chicken Salad

A flavor-packed riff on a classic, this Thai chicken salad makes a refreshing change as a lunchtime entree.

Servings: 4 • **Prep time:** 15 mins.

Ingredients

- ¾ cup plain Greek yogurt
- ¼ cup mayonnaise
- 2 teaspoons sriracha
- 1 stalk lemongrass (about 2–3 inches long), with outer covering removed
- Splash of rice wine vinegar
- White and dark meat of 1 whole roasted chicken, shredded or cubed
- ½ cup red cabbage, julienned
- ¼ cup fresh Thai basil, chopped
- 2 teaspoons sesame seeds
- Sea salt and cracked pepper, to taste
- Bean sprouts (optional)
- Serve with lettuce leaves and avocadoes, sliced

1. In a medium bowl, combine the yogurt, mayonnaise, sriracha, lemongrass, and vinegar. Mix well, occasionally bruising the lemongrass with your whisk to release its flavor. Set the mixture aside.
2. In a large bowl, combine the remaining ingredients and stir until well combined. Remove the lemongrass stalk from the yogurt mixture and add the mixture to the chicken salad. Stir well. Enjoy cold, on a large leaf of lettuce with a slice of avocado.

Carrot "Soufflé"

Traditional soufflés rely on the air trapped in whipped egg whites for their height. This cheat recipe uses some baking powder to help the mixture rise and saves you time and energy while still achieving a light, airy texture.

Servings: 4-6 • **Prep time:** 10 mins. • **Cook time:** 1 hr.

Ingredients

- 2 pounds carrots, chopped
- 4 eggs
- ⅔ cup sugar
- ½ cup butter
- ¼ cup flour
- 2 teaspoons vanilla extract
- 1½ teaspoons baking powder
- ½ teaspoon salt
- ½ teaspoon cinnamon
- ¼ teaspoon nutmeg
- Garnish: confectioner's sugar, sifted

1. Preheat the oven to 350°F. Coat a casserole dish with baking spray.
2. Place 1 quart of water over high heat and bring it to a boil. Add the carrots and boil for 15 minutes, or until the carrots are tender. Transfer the carrots to a blender or food processor and process until smooth, about 2 minutes, scraping down the side of the bowl as necessary. Add the remaining ingredients to the blender and blend until smooth.
3. Pour the mixture into the casserole dish and bake for 40–45 minutes, until the top is golden brown. Top the soufflé with sifted confectioner's sugar and serve warm or at room temperature.

Carrot Curry Bisque

The potent combination of carrots, curry, ginger, and garlic in this comforting bisque offers an impressive list of micronutrients and phytochemicals that help with everything from blood sugar management to disease prevention.

Servings: 8 • **Prep time:** 7–10 mins. • **Cook time:** 45–55 mins.

Ingredients

- 3 tablespoons olive oil
- 1 onion, chopped
- 6 carrots, chopped
- 4 whole parsnips, cleaned with tops removed
- 4 cloves garlic, minced
- 1 (13.6 ounce) can coconut milk
- 2 teaspoons curry powder
- 1 teaspoon fresh ginger, grated
- 6 cups vegetable stock
- 2 tablespoons maple syrup
- 1½ teaspoons salt
- ¾ teaspoon cayenne pepper
- Garnish: cilantro, chopped

1. Heat the oil in a large pot over medium heat. Add the onion and cook for 5 minutes. Add in the carrots and parsnips and cook for 5 minutes, stirring frequently. Add the garlic and sauté for 45 seconds, until fragrant.
2. Add the remaining ingredients. Cook on medium heat until boiling, then reduce the heat to a simmer and simmer for 20–30 minutes, until all the vegetables are very tender.
3. Using an immersion blender or food processor, blend the soup until smooth. If you're using a food processor, let the soup cool slightly and work in batches to achieve a smoother consistency. Serve the bisque hot or cold, garnished with chopped cilantro.

Italian Wedding Soup

The union between Italian sausage and freshly-picked greens is the real marriage behind minestra maritata. Consider high-quality chicken stock and Parmigiano Reggiano to be the best man and maid of honor. In this dish, pasta is the fifth bridesmaid you could leave out in a pinch.

Servings: 8 • **Prep time:** 15 mins. • **Cook time:** 20 mins.

Ingredients
For the meatballs

- 1 tablespoon olive oil
- 1 shallot, minced
- 1 pound Italian sausage
- 1 large egg
- ¼ cup breadcrumbs
- ½ cup Parmigiano Reggiano
- 1 teaspoon salt
- ½ teaspoon freshly ground black pepper
- 2 cloves garlic, minced
- 3 tablespoons fresh parsley, chopped

For the soup

- 1 tablespoon olive oil
- 1 medium onion, chopped
- 2 carrots, peeled and chopped
- 1 parsnip, peeled and chopped
- 4 cloves garlic, minced
- 1 cup escarole or kale, torn
- 1 cup acini de pepe or orzo pasta
- 8 cups chicken stock
- 2 teaspoons salt
- 1 teaspoon freshly ground pepper
- Serve with ½ cup Parmigiano Reggiano and ¼ cup fresh parsley, chopped

1. To begin making the meatballs, in a large stockpot, heat the oil over medium heat. Combine all the remaining ingredients for the meatballs into a large ball using your hands, mixing until well combined. Roll the mixture into meatballs, about 1¼ inches in diameter. Cook for 5 minutes on each side, until golden brown. Transfer them to a paper towel–lined plate with a slotted spoon.
2. To make the soup, add the oil to the same pot. Add the onions, carrots, and parsnips and sauté for 3 minutes. Add the garlic and cook for 1 minute. Add the greens, pasta, chicken stock, salt, and pepper. Increase the heat to high until the soup reaches a rolling boil, about 5 minutes. Spoon in the meatballs and decrease the heat to a simmer.
3. Cover the soup and cook for 5 minutes to allow the flavors to marry. Serve with Parmigiano Reggiano and fresh parsley.

Spinach Alfredo Pizza with Cauliflower Crust

Cauliflower has become a favorite stand-in for meat, flour, and, sometimes, pretty much any food people are afraid to eat. In particular, cauliflower pizza crust has become a favorite low-carb option in my house.

Serving: one 14-inch pizza • **Prep time:** 20 mins. • **Cook time:** 50 mins.

Ingredients

- 1 head cauliflower, washed, with leaves and stem removed
- 1 egg
- ¼ cup Parmigiano Reggiano, shredded
- ¼ cup shredded mozzarella, plus 1 cup
- 1 teaspoon dried oregano
- 1 teaspoon dried basil
- ½ teaspoon salt, plus more to taste
- ¼ teaspoon ground pepper, plus more to taste
- 2 tablespoons olive oil
- 4 ounces boneless, skinless chicken breast, cut in half lengthwise
- 2 cloves garlic, minced
- ½ cup alfredo sauce
- 1 cup spinach, chopped
- ¼ cup tomato, chopped
- Garnishes: red pepper flakes, bacon crumbles (optional)

1. Preheat the oven to 375°F. Line a baking sheet with parchment paper.
2. Pulse the cauliflower in a blender or food processor for 2–3 minutes, until finely ground. Spread the ground cauliflower evenly onto the parchment-lined baking sheet and bake for 15 minutes.
3. Once cooled, transfer the cauliflower to a medium bowl lined with cheesecloth or a clean kitchen towel. Strain the liquid from the cauliflower by squeezing it through the cheesecloth. Repeatedly squeeze the cheesecloth until you feel like you can squeeze no more. Now, squeeze three more times to remove any remaining liquid.
4. Increase the oven temperature to 450°F. Line the baking sheet with new parchment paper and coat it with nonstick cooking spray.
5. Transfer the cauliflower to a large bowl and add the egg, Parmigiano Reggiano, mozzarella, dried herbs, salt, and pepper. Stir until well combined and shape the mixture into a ball with your hands. Transfer the dough to the parchment-lined baking sheet. Using your fingers or a spatula, spread the dough until a 14-inch round is formed.
6. Bake the crust for 15 minutes, until golden brown, and carefully flip the crust over using a large spatula. Bake for 5–7 minutes, until both sides are browned and the crust is crisp.

7. While the crust bakes, heat the olive oil in a sauté pan over medium heat. Once the oil is hot and starts to shimmer, add the chicken breast and season it with salt and pepper. When the chicken has begun to brown (about 3 minutes), flip it and cook the other side for 2–3 minutes, until golden brown. Remove the chicken from the pan and chop it into bite-size cubes. Add the minced garlic to the sauté pan and sauté for 1 minute before adding the alfredo sauce and the chicken back into the pan. Scraping the bottom of the pan, bring the sauce to a simmer. Once simmering, add in the spinach and tomato. Remove the pan from the heat immediately when the spinach has started to wilt.

8. Spoon the alfredo sauce mixture onto the pizza crust until it is evenly distributed. Top the sauce with 1 cup of mozzarella. Bake the pizza for 5–7 minutes, until the cheese has melted and begins to golden.

9. Remove the pizza from the oven and cut into 8 slices. Top with red pepper flakes and/or bacon crumbles prior to enjoying.

Five Variations on Pesto

The basic flavor building blocks of pesto are garlic, pine nuts, basil, and hard cheese like Parmigiano Reggiano, but you can swap these ingredients with other nuts, herbs, and cheeses to create something completely new!

Radish Leaf Pesto

Makes: 2½ cups • **Prep time:** 5 mins.

Ingredients

- 2 cups radish leaves, rinsed and stemmed
- ½ cup toasted pistachios
- 2 cloves garlic
- Juice and zest of 1 lemon
- ¼ cup Parmigiano Reggiano
- ½ teaspoon sea salt
- ¼ teaspoon red pepper flakes
- ½ cup olive oil

1. Place all the ingredients except for the olive oil in a food processor and blend until a paste is formed.
2. While the blender is on, drizzle the olive oil into the feed tube. Taste and adjust the seasonings as desired.

Traditional Pesto

Makes: 2½ cups • **Prep time:** 5 mins.

Ingredients

- 2 cups fresh basil
- ½ cup raw unsalted pine nuts
- 2 cloves garlic
- Juice and zest of 1 lemon
- ¼ cup Parmigiano Reggiano
- ½ teaspoon sea salt
- ¼ teaspoon freshly ground black pepper
- ½ cup olive oil

1. Place all the ingredients except for the olive oil in a food processor and blend until a paste is formed.
2. While the blender is on, drizzle the olive oil into the feed tube. Taste and adjust the seasonings as desired.

Carrot Top Pesto

Makes: 2½ cups • **Prep time:** 5 mins.

Ingredients

- 2 cups carrot-top greens, rinsed
- ½ cup raw unsalted walnuts
- 2 cloves garlic
- Juice and zest of 1 lemon
- ¼ cup goat cheese
- ½ teaspoon sea salt
- ¼ teaspoon freshly ground black pepper
- ½ cup olive oil

1. Place all the ingredients except for the olive oil in a food processor and blend until a paste is formed.
2. While the blender is on, drizzle the olive oil into the feed tube. Taste and adjust the seasonings as desired.

Celery Leaf Pesto

Makes: 2½ cups • **Prep time:** 5 mins.

Ingredients

- 2 cups celery leaves, rinsed
- ½ cup raw unsalted almonds
- 2 cloves garlic
- Juice and zest of 1 lemon
- ¼ cup cheddar
- ½ teaspoon sea salt
- ¼ teaspoon freshly ground black pepper
- ½ bell pepper, sliced
- ½ cup olive oil

1. Place all the ingredients except for the olive oil in a food processor and blend until a paste is formed.
2. While the blender is on, drizzle the olive oil into the feed tube. Taste and adjust the seasonings as desired.

Mustard Leaf Pesto

Makes: 2½ cups • **Prep time:** 5 mins.

Ingredients

- 2 cups mustard leaves, chopped
- ½ cup raw unsalted cashews
- 2 cloves garlic
- Juice and zest of 1 lemon
- ¼ cup Parmigiano Reggiano
- ½ teaspoon sea salt
- 4 ounces cream cheese
- ½ cup olive oil

1. Place all the ingredients except for the olive oil in a food processor and blend until a paste is formed.
2. While the blender is on, drizzle the olive oil into the feed tube. Taste and adjust the seasonings as desired.

ABOUT THE AUTHOR

Kayla Butts, MS, RDN, LD is a sixth generation Texan, small-scale farmer, full-time dietitian, and mom to three strong girls. Along with being the author of *Garden to Table Cookbook*, she's also written over 100 magazine features and articles published throughout the state of Texas.

As the daughter of a single mom putting herself through school while working full time, Kayla grew up on Happy Meals and Chef Boyardee. After seeing her mother's epilepsy successfully treated with food, Kayla became determined to help people prevent and treat disease through the way they eat.

She holds a master's degree in nutrition and has been a practicing dietitian nutritionist for 15 years, helping hundreds of clients meet their nutrition-focused health goals. Today, as a recipe developer and food stylist, she creates simple, seasonal recipes using ingredients from her own garden.

Dedications

"For my family, my reasons why." —Kayla

"To my Father in heaven, I would not be the person I am without You. To my family, thank you for your love and encouragement."—Rachel

CREDITS

1. Loprinzi PD, Branscum A, Hanks J. (2016) Healthy Lifestyle Characteristics and Their Joint Association With Cardiovascular Disease Biomarkers in US Adults. Mayo Clinic Proceedings. 2016 April;91(4):432-442. https://doi.org/10.1016/j.mayocp.2016.01.009

2. FAO and ITPS. (2015) Status of the World's Soil Resources (SWSR) – Main Report. Food and Agriculture Organization of the United Nations and Intergovernmental Technical Panel on Soils, Rome, Italy https://www.fao.org/3/i5199e/i5199e.pdf

3. Gupta S. (2007) If We are What We Eat, Americans are Corn and Soy. CNN Health Online. https://www.cnn.com/2007/HEALTH/diet.fitness/09/22/kd.gupta.column/

4. Davis DR, Epp MD, Riordan HD. (2004) Changes in USDA Food Composition Data For 43 Garden Crops, 1950 to 1999. J Am Coll Nutr. 2004 Dec;23(6):669-82. doi: 10.1080/07315724.2004.10719409. PMID: 15637215.

5. Scheer R, Moss D. (2011) Dirt Poor: Have Fruits and Vegetables Become Less Nutritious? Scientific American Online. https://www.scientificamerican.com/article/soil-depletion-and-nutrition-loss/

6. Thomas DE. (2000) A Study on the Mineral Depletion of the Foods Available to Us as a Nation Over the Period 1940 to 1991. http://www.mineralresourcesint.co.uk/pdf/mineral_deplet.pdf.

7. Ozlu E, Kumar S. (2018) Response of Soil Organic Carbon, pH, Electrical Conductivity, and Water Stable Aggregates to Long-Term Annual Manure and Inorganic Fertilizer. Soil Science Society of America Journal, 82: 1243-1251. https://doi.org/10.2136/sssaj2018.02.0082

8. Triguero-Mas M, Anguelovski I, Cirac-Claveras J, Connolly J, Vazquez A, Urgell-Plaza F, et al. (2020) Quality of Life Benefits of Urban Rooftop Gardening for People With Intellectual Disabilities or Mental Health Disorders. Prev Chronic Dis 2020;17:200087. DOI: http://dx.doi.org/10.5888/pcd17.200087

9. Journal of Health Psychology 3.231 Impact Factor 5-Year Impact Factor 3.297 Journal Indexing & Metrics » Gardening Promotes Neuroendocrine and Affective Restoration from Stress Agnes E. Van Den Berg, Mariëtte H.G. Custers First Published June 3, 2010 Research Article Find in PubMed https://doi.org/10.1177/1359105310365577

10. Gonzalez MT, Hartig T, Patil GG, Martinsen EW, Kirkevold M. (2011) A Prospective Study of Group Cohesiveness in Therapeutic Horticulture for Clinical Depression. International Journal of Mental Health Nursing, 20: 119-129. https://doi.org/10.1111/j.1447-0349.2010.00689.x

11. Berger P, Berger TW. (2017) The use of Sensory Perception of Plants in Horticultural Therapy of Alcohol Addiction. Journal of Therapeutic Horticulture. Volume XXVII. Issue 11. P 1-19

12. Decker KP, Peglow SL & Samples CR. (2014) Participation in a Novel Treatment Component during Residential Substance Use Treatment is Associated with Improved Outcome: a Pilot Study. Addict Sci Clin Pract 9, 7. https://doi.org/10.1186/1940-0640-9-7

13. Simons LA, Simons J, McCallum J, Friedlander Y. (2006) Lifestyle factors and risk of dementia: Dubbo Study of the elderly. Med J Aust. Jan 16;184(2):68-70. doi: 10.5694/j.1326-5377.2006.tb00120.x. PMID: 16411871.

14. Tu HM, Chiu PY. (2020) Meta-analysis of controlled trials testing horticultural therapy for the improvement of cognitive function. Sci Rep 10, 14637. https://doi.org/10.1038/s41598-020-71621-7

15. Lim Wong GC, Kheng Siang Ng T, Le Lee J, et al. (2021) Horticultural Therapy Reduces Biomarkers of Immunosenescence and Inflammaging in Community-Dwelling Older Adults: A Feasibility Pilot Randomized Controlled Trial, The Journals of Gerontology: Series A, Volume 76, Issue 2, February 2021, Pages 307–317, https://doi.org/10.1093/gerona/glaa271

16. De Rui M, Toffanello ED, Veronese N, Zambon S, Bolzetta F, Sartori L, et al. (2014) Vitamin D Deficiency and Leisure Time Activities in the Elderly: Are All Pastimes the Same? PLoS ONE 9(4): e94805. https://doi.org/10.1371/journal.pone.0094805

17. Hoel DG, Berwick M, de Gruijl FR, Holick MF. (2016) The Risks and Benefits of Sun Exposure. Dermatoendocrinol. 2016 Oct 19;8(1):e1248325. doi: 10.1080/19381980.2016.1248325. PMID: 27942349; PMCID: PMC5129901.

18. Center for Disease Control and Prevention, (2022) Physical Activity for a Healthy Weight. Healthy Weight, Nutrition, and Physical Activity. CDC ²⅘. https://www.cdc.gov/healthyweight/physical_activity/index.html?s_cid=tw_ob387

19. Chevalier G, Sinatra ST, Oschman JL, Sokal K, Sokal P. (2012) Earthing: Health Implications of Reconnecting the Human Body to the Earth's Surface Electrons, Journal of Environmental and Public Health, vol. 2012, Article ID 291541, 8 pages. https://doi.org/10.1155/2012/291541

INDEX